CONCISE
Britain

G000294976

Contents

II	Key to road map symbols
III	Distance table
IV	Counties map
1	Key to map pages
2	Road maps of Great Britain at 8 miles to 1 inch
58	Road maps of Ireland at 19 miles to 1 inch
62	Index to road maps of Ireland
64	Index to road maps of Great Britain

www.philips-maps.co.uk

First published in 2010 by Philip's
a division of Octopus Publishing Group Ltd
www.octopusbooks.co.uk
Endeavour House, 189 Shaftesbury Avenue
London WC2H 8JY
An Hachette UK Company
www.hachette.co.uk

First edition 2010, second impression 2011

ISBN 978-1-84907-070-6

Cartography by Philip's, copyright © 2010 Philip's

No part of this publication may be reproduced, stored in a retrieval system or transmitted in any form or by any means, electronic, mechanical, photocopying, recording or otherwise, without the permission of the Publishers and the copyright owner.

While every reasonable effort has been made to ensure that the information compiled in this atlas is accurate, complete and up-to-date at the time of publication, some of this information is subject to change and the Publisher cannot guarantee its correctness or completeness.

The information in this atlas is provided without any representation or warranty, express or implied and the Publisher cannot be held liable for any loss or damage due to any use or reliance on the information in this atlas, nor for any errors, omissions or subsequent changes in such information.

The representation in this atlas of any road, drive or track is no evidence of the existence of a right of way.

The map of Ireland on pages 58–61 is based on Ordnance Survey Ireland by permisson of the Government Permit Number 8704 © Ordnance Survey Ireland and Government of Ireland and

Ordnance Survey Northern Ireland on behalf of the Controller of Her Majesty's Stationery Office © Crown copyright 2010 Permit Number 100141.

Printed in China

*Independent research survey, from research carried out by Outlook Research Limited, 2005/06.
**Estimated sales of all Phiip's UK road atlases since launch.

Road map symbols

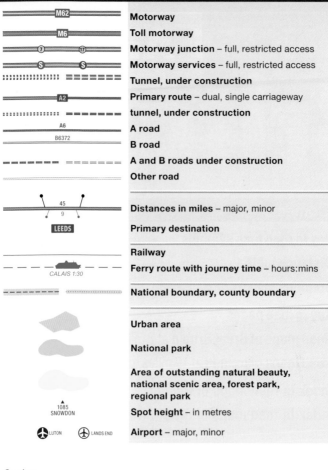

Motorway

Toll motorway

Motorway junction – full, restricted access

Motorway services – full, restricted access

Tunnel, under construction

Primary route – dual, single carriageway

tunnel, under construction

A road

B road

A and B roads under construction

Other road

Distances in miles – major, minor

Primary destination

Railway

Ferry route with journey time – hours:mins

National boundary, county boundary

Urban area

National park

Area of outstanding natural beauty, national scenic area, forest park, regional park

Spot height – in metres

Airport – major, minor

Abbreviated local authority areas

BD	Bridgend	13 G12
BF	Bracknell Forest	16 J3
BG	Blaenau Gwent	13 E15
BL	Blackpool	26 B4
BM	Bournemouth	8 H5
BN	Blackburn with Darwen	27 C8
CB	City and County of Bristol	14 J4
CBH	City of Brighton and Hove	10 J3
CE	City of Edinburgh	40 F5
CF	Cardiff	7 C10
CM	Clackmannanshire	40 D2
CN	City of Nottingham	22 A4
CY	Caerphilly	7 B10
DD	Dundee City	51 P3
DE	Derby City	22 B2
DN	Darlington	32 C4
ED	East Dunbartonshire	39 C11
ER	East Renfrewshire	39 E9
FK	Falkirk	39 C13
GC	Glasgow City	39 D10
HL	Hartlepool	32 A6
HN	Halton	26 G6
IC	Inverclyde	39 D8
KH	Kingston upon Hull	29 A9
LE	Leicester City	22 E5
LU	Luton	16 C5
MB	Middlesbrough	32 C6
MR	Merthyr Tydfil	13 E14
NEL	North East Lincolnshire	29 D11
NL	North Lanarkshire	39 D13
NP	Newport	7 C12
NPT	Neath Port Talbot	13 F12
PL	Plymouth	3 F12
PM	Portsmouth	9 G11
PO	Poole	8 H5
RC	Redcar and Cleveland	33 C8
RD	Reading	16 H2
RF	Renfrewshire	39 D9
RT	Rhondda Cynon Taff	7 B9
SD	Southend-on-Sea	17 G14
SL	Slough	16 G4
SN	Stockton-on-Tees	32 B6
SO	Southampton	9 F9
ST	Stoke-on-Trent	21 A9
SW	Swindon	15 G10
TB	Torbay	4 G2
TF	Torfaen	7 A11
TK	Thurrock	17 G12
TW	Telford and Wrekin	20 E7
WA	Warrington	26 G7
WD	West Dunbartonshire	39 C9
WK	Wokingham	16 J2
WL	West Lothian	40 F3
WM	Windsor and Maidenhead	16 H3

Scales

Pages 2–56

1:506880, 1cm = 5.07 km, 1 in = 8 miles

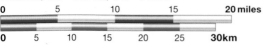

Pages 58–61

1:1200000, 1cm = 12km, 1 in = 18.94 miles

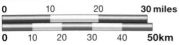

Distance table

How to use this table

Distances are shown in miles and, in light type, kilometres. For example, the distance between Birmingham and Dover is **194** miles or 312 kilometres.

London

	Miles (bold) / kilometres (light)
Aberdeen	517 / 832
Aberystwyth	211 445 / 340 716
Birmingham	117 420 114 / 188 676 183
Bournemouth	107 564 207 147 / 172 908 333 237
Brighton	52 573 253 163 92 / 84 922 407 262 148
Bristol	122 493 125 81 82 147 / 196 793 201 130 132 237
Cambridge	54 471 214 100 154 116 169 / 87 758 344 161 248 187 272
Cardiff	157 505 105 103 117 182 45 190 / 253 813 169 166 188 293 72 306
Carlisle	301 221 224 196 343 370 277 264 289 / 484 356 360 315 552 596 446 425 465
Dover	71 588 297 194 174 82 202 125 238 389 / 114 947 478 312 280 132 325 201 383 626
Dundee	448 67 376 349 495 517 430 406 441 152 523 / 721 108 605 562 797 832 692 654 710 245 842
Edinburgh	390 125 320 292 439 456 373 345 385 96 462 56 / 628 201 515 470 707 734 600 555 620 154 744 90
Fishguard	260 504 56 170 222 291 154 270 112 297 331 460 399 / 418 811 90 274 357 468 248 435 180 478 533 740 642
Fort William	510 149 430 392 539 575 486 479 485 206 596 127 144 486 / 821 240 692 631 867 926 782 771 781 332 959 204 232 782
Glasgow	397 145 320 292 439 468 373 372 385 96 488 83 44 376 101 / 639 233 515 470 707 753 600 599 620 154 786 134 71 605 163
Gloucester	109 468 102 56 99 159 35 123 56 247 191 410 349 153 454 346 / 175 753 164 90 159 256 56 198 90 398 307 660 562 246 731 557
Harwich	76 535 281 167 187 128 217 67 246 336 125 469 413 337 543 432 196 / 122 861 452 269 301 206 349 108 396 541 201 755 665 542 874 695 316
Holyhead	269 491 111 148 288 334 206 270 216 231 360 394 333 167 438 330 191 349 / 433 790 179 238 463 538 332 435 348 372 580 634 536 269 705 531 307 562
Inverness	550 105 486 458 597 617 539 505 549 262 622 132 158 542 66 166 504 569 474 / 885 169 782 737 961 993 867 813 884 422 1001 212 254 872 106 267 811 916 763
John o' Groats	663 232 601 574 724 741 668 630 680 391 746 259 285 671 195 295 628 693 603 129 / 1067 373 967 924 1165 1193 1075 1014 1094 629 1201 417 459 1080 314 475 1011 1116 970 208
Kingston upon Hull	184 364 223 134 264 245 233 139 244 158 256 295 234 280 369 254 169 196 231 394 518 / 296 586 359 216 425 394 375 224 393 254 412 475 377 450 594 409 272 316 372 634 834
Land's End	297 692 313 281 205 308 200 374 245 477 381 642 574 353 686 573 235 390 405 741 868 421 / 478 1114 504 452 330 496 322 602 394 768 613 1033 924 568 1104 922 378 628 652 1193 1397 678
Leeds	189 327 169 113 255 260 194 145 232 119 260 258 202 237 329 215 174 223 176 360 487 55 405 / 304 526 272 182 410 419 312 233 373 192 418 415 325 381 530 346 280 359 283 579 784 89 652
Lincoln	131 383 199 90 209 197 183 85 208 191 202 314 258 272 399 291 159 155 216 427 554 44 371 68 / 211 616 320 145 336 317 295 137 335 307 325 505 415 438 642 468 256 249 348 687 892 71 597 109
Liverpool	202 341 104 93 234 272 161 194 169 120 299 286 216 160 329 216 140 265 102 382 511 130 361 75 129 / 325 549 167 150 377 438 259 312 272 193 481 460 348 257 530 348 225 427 164 615 822 209 581 121 208
Manchester	185 340 129 80 227 257 161 165 183 119 276 285 215 197 329 215 126 228 124 373 500 95 361 40 84 35 / 298 547 208 129 365 414 259 266 295 192 444 459 346 317 530 346 203 367 200 600 805 153 581 64 135 56
Newcastle upon Tyne	286 235 257 207 347 352 299 241 325 57 358 166 110 329 253 148 266 308 272 268 395 132 498 92 159 168 132 / 460 378 414 333 558 567 481 388 523 92 576 267 177 529 407 238 428 496 438 431 636 212 802 148 256 270 212
Norwich	114 496 276 166 214 175 252 62 262 289 174 422 366 343 504 385 204 73 311 529 654 149 421 176 105 220 185 264 / 183 798 444 267 344 282 406 100 422 465 280 679 589 552 811 620 328 117 501 852 1053 240 678 283 169 354 298 425
Oxford	57 483 154 64 90 108 74 83 108 260 141 433 372 205 472 356 52 145 238 532 656 192 274 168 137 172 144 260 145 / 92 777 248 103 145 174 119 134 174 418 227 697 599 330 760 573 84 233 383 856 1056 309 441 270 221 277 232 418 233
Plymouth	218 615 237 203 128 224 122 293 167 399 300 547 496 264 595 495 157 309 328 664 790 355 89 316 293 283 283 410 343 199 / 351 990 382 327 206 361 196 472 269 642 483 880 798 425 958 797 253 497 528 1069 1271 571 143 509 472 455 455 660 552 320
Sheffield	159 360 159 76 216 226 161 120 194 152 245 291 235 215 348 248 126 187 168 393 520 65 361 33 46 72 38 125 146 135 283 / 256 579 256 122 348 364 259 193 312 245 394 468 378 346 560 399 203 301 270 632 837 105 581 53 74 116 61 201 235 217 455
Southampton	77 547 201 128 31 61 76 148 121 324 143 500 438 233 541 433 105 164 293 598 723 256 228 232 204 239 221 324 206 64 151 199 / 124 880 323 206 50 98 122 238 195 521 230 805 705 375 871 697 169 264 472 963 1164 412 367 373 328 385 356 521 332 103 243 320
Stranraer	402 228 325 297 444 475 378 379 390 101 496 167 124 392 195 84 343 410 338 262 379 259 585 220 298 221 220 185 403 379 500 263 445 / 647 367 523 478 715 765 608 610 628 163 798 269 200 631 314 135 552 660 544 422 610 417 942 354 480 356 354 298 649 610 805 423 716
Swansea	194 507 73 119 167 222 85 227 41 309 274 473 412 67 496 409 89 267 184 572 696 264 177 248 233 195 187 347 301 328 206 217 161 417 / 312 816 117 192 269 357 137 365 66 497 441 761 663 108 798 658 143 430 296 921 1120 425 285 399 375 314 301 559 485 527 332 349 259 671
York	207 319 195 130 269 275 222 165 244 121 282 250 194 261 330 217 189 228 204 352 479 37 411 24 75 99 64 84 181 181 333 52 258 222 272 / 333 513 314 209 433 443 357 266 393 195 454 402 312 420 531 349 304 367 328 566 771 60 661 39 121 159 103 135 291 291 536 84 415 357 438

(Map of Great Britain with the following locations labelled:) John o' Groats, Inverness, Aberdeen, Fort William, Dundee, Glasgow, Edinburgh, Stranraer, Newcastle upon Tyne, Carlisle, Leeds, York, Kingston upon Hull, Manchester, Lincoln, Holyhead, Liverpool, Sheffield, Norwich, Birmingham, Aberystwyth, Cambridge, Fishguard, Gloucester, Oxford, Harwich, Swansea, Cardiff, Bristol, London, Dover, Southampton, Brighton, Bournemouth, Plymouth, Land's End

Counties and unitary authorities

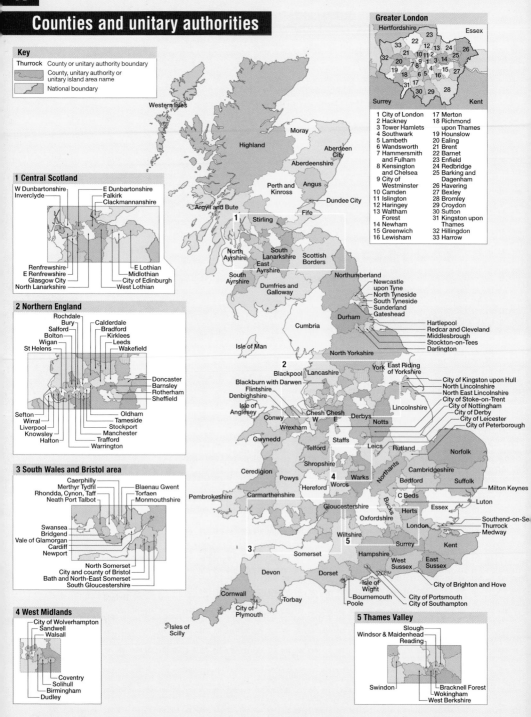

Key to map pages

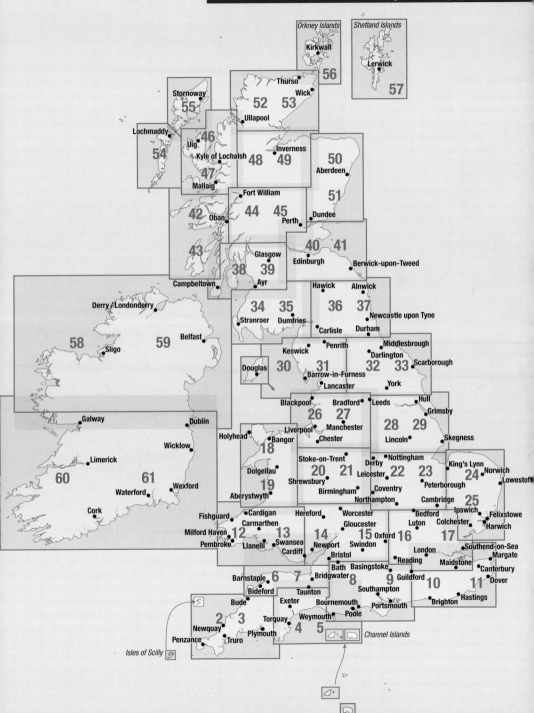

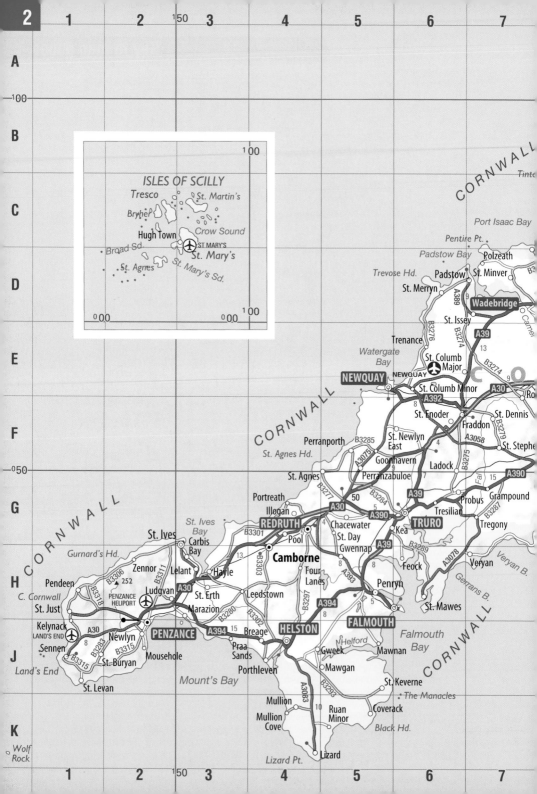

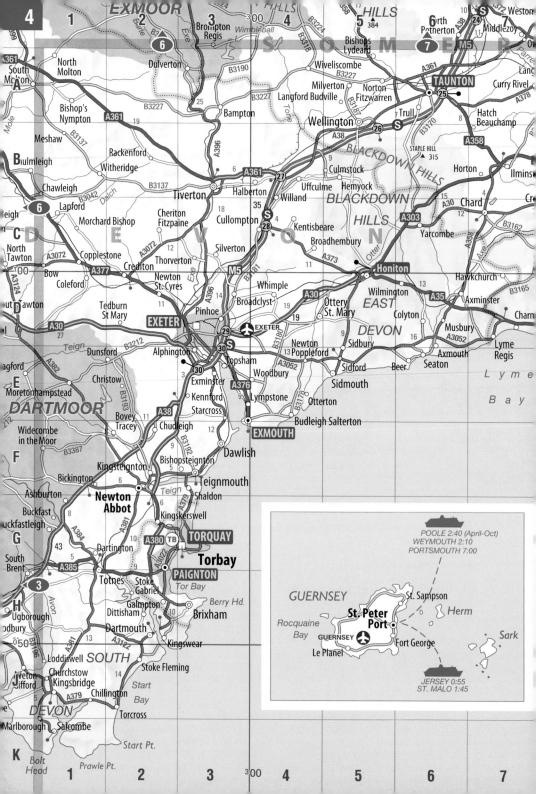

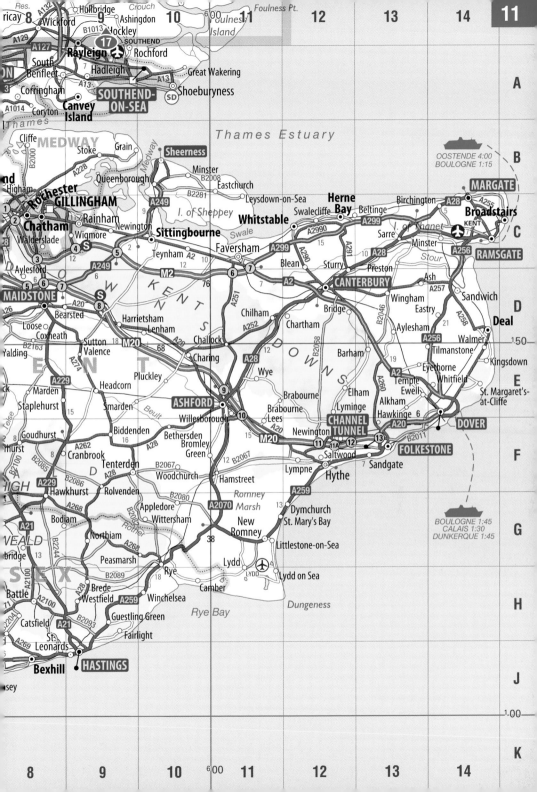

WARWICKSHIRE

Feckenham · Astwood Bank · Studley · Wootton Wawen · Southam · Stockton · Daventry · Weedon Bec
Inkberrow · Alcester · A46 Barford · Harbury · ARBURY HILL 224
Upton Snodsbury · Bidford-on-Avon · Wellesbourne · Fenny Compton · Byfield
Salford Priors · STRATFORD-UPON-AVON · Gaydon · Kineton · M40
Harvington · Cleeve Prior · Ettington · Wardington
EVESHAM · Halford · Wroxton · Middleton Cheney
Bretforton · ILMINGTON DOWNS 260 · Shipston-on-Stour · BANBURY · King's Sutton · Brackley
Eckington · Ashton under Hill · Mickleton · Swalcliffe · Aynho
BREDON HILL 293 · Chipping Campden · Bloxham · Ardley
Broadway · Blockley · Moreton-in-Marsh · Long Compton · Deddington · Middle Barton · Upper Heyford
Ashchurch · Stanway · Hook Norton · Middleton · Kirtlington · Bicester
Bishop's Cleeve · Winchcombe · Chipping Norton · Enstone · Charlbury · Ambrosden
CLEEVE CLOUD · Prestbury · Stow-on-the-Wold · Churchill · Charlbury · Woodstock · Bletchingdon
CHELTENHAM · COTSWOLDS · Bourton-on-the-Water · Shipton under Wychwood · Kidlington · Islip
Charlton Kings · Andoversford · Burford · Witney · Yarnton · Stanton St. John
Withington · Northleach · Aldsworth · Brize Norton · Eynsham · Botley · OXFORD · Wheatley
North Cerney · Bibury · Carterton · Stanton Harcourt · Cumnor · Kennington
Stratton · CIRENCESTER · Fairford · Bampton · Standlake · Sandleigh · Radley
South Cerney · Lechlade-on-Thames · Buckland · Kingston Bagpuize · Abingdon
Kemble · Cricklade · Highworth · Faringdon · Dorchester · Sutton Courtenay · Benson
Ashton Keynes · Minety · Watchfield · Grove · Harwell · Didcot · Blewbury · Cholsey
Charlton · Purton · Shrivenham · Uffington · Wantage
Brinkworth · Stratton St. Margaret · Ashbury · WHITE HORSE HILL 261 · Farnborough · East Ilsley · Streatley
SWINDON · Wanborough · Lambourn · Compton · Pangbourne
Great Somerford · Wootton Bassett · Wroughton · BERKSHIRE DOWNS · Hampstead Norreys
M4 · Lyneham · Chiseldon · Aldbourne · Great Shefford · Welford · Hermitage · Theale
CHIPPENHAM · NORTH WESSEX · Ogbourne St. George · Whitonditch · Hungerford · NEWBURY
Calne · Broad Hinton · Avebury · Froxfield · WEST BERKSHIRE
Hilmarton · Cherhill · MARLBOROUGH · WALBURY HILL 297 · Thatcham · Heath End
Lacock · Bromham · Beckhampton · TAN HILL 294 · East Woodhay · Burghclere
Melksham · Devizes · Pewsey · Burbage · WEST BERKSHIRE

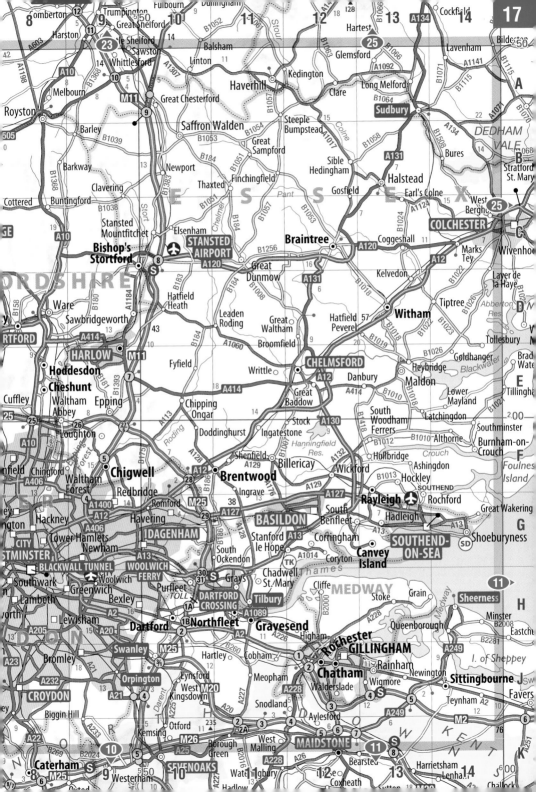

Leven

Skirlaugh
Aldbrough

Beverley
33
A1035
A165

North Newbald
A1079
B1248

orth

South Cave

North

Cottingham
KH
Sproatley
B1238
B1242

HOLDERNESS

KINGSTON UPON HULL
Marfleet
Preston
Hedon
B1362
Withernsea

Hessle
Paull
Burstwick
Hollym

HUMBER BRIDGE
A1033
Keyingham
Patrington

North Ferriby
New Holland
A1033
B1445

Barton upon Humber
Barrow upon Humber
Humber
Sunk Island
Easington

Winterton
B1206
A1077
Ulceby
A160
Immingham
Kilnsea

Bonby
B1204
A15
Stallingborough

SCUNTHORPE
5
Broughton
A18
Keelby
A180
GRIMSBY
Cleethorpes
Spurn Hd.

4
Barnetby le Wold
A1084
HUMBERSIDE
Laceby

Brigg
Waltham
Humberston
Mouth of the Humber

ROTTERDAM 10:25
ZEEBRUGGE 10:25

Hibaldstow
Grasby
A1173
A18
New Waltham
NEL
Tetney

Caenby Corner
Waddingham
B1434
A46
Caistor Nettleton
A16
Marshchapel
Donna Nook
400

West Rasen
Usselby
Normanby le Wold
Binbrook
North Thoresby
Ludborough
Grainthorpe
North Somercotes
Saltfleet

Market Rasen
A631
Saltfleetby

Faldingworth
Ludford
South Elkington
Louth
Manby
A1031
Mablethorpe

Hainton
B1225
A157
Legbourne
Withern
Sutton-on-Sea

LINCOLNSHIRE WOLDS

Welton
A46
Stainton
Wragby
Scamblesby
A16
Maltby le Marsh
Huttoft

LINCOLNSHIRE

Nettleham
A158
Belchford
Ulceby Cross
A1104
Alford
Chapel St. Leonards

LINCOLN
A57
Washingborough
Bardney
A158
Horncastle
Hagworthingham
A1028
Willoughby
A52
Ingoldmells

North Hykeham
Branston
B1190
Woodhall Spa
Old Bolingbroke
Partney
Spilsby
A158
Burgh le Marsh
SKEGNESS

Waddington
Bracebridge Heath
Metheringham
Mareham le Fen
B1195
Wainfleet All Saints

Scopwick
Coningsby
Stickford
Steeping
Gibraltar Pt.

Navenby
A15
Digby
Walcott
Stickney
A16
East Fen

Welbourn
A607
Billinghay
A153
West Fen
Sibsey
A52
Wrangle

Cranwell
Ruskington
B1192
B1183
Old Leake
350

Leasingham
Sleaford
23
Brothertoft
Holland Fen
23
ton
BOSTON

Ancaster
A17
Heckingt
A1121
A52
Fishtoft

Honington
8 9 10 11 12 13 14

Map content

Isle of Whithorn

34

35

WORKINGTON

Maryport
Fothergill
Crosby
Bothel
Ellen
Dearham
26
Derwe
Flimby
Seaton
Cockermouth
Great Clifton
A66
A595
Bassenthwa
Harrington
8
13
Distington
Parton
A5086
Thornth
B52
WHITEHAVEN
St. Bee's Hd.
Frizington
Cleator Moor
Crummock
Water
LA
St. Bees
4
Egremont
Ennerdale
Water
Bu
DIST
Beckermet
Calder Bridge
Wast Water
NATI
Sellafield
A595
Gosforth
Boc
Seascale
Irt
PA
Drigg
28
Esk
Ravenglass
Bootle
BLACK
COMBE
600
A59
Whicham
A5093
K
Mj
Haverigg
Dalton-in-Fu
BARROW-IN-FURNESS
Vickerstown
I. of Walney
Hilpsfore

Isle of Man inset

ISLE OF MAN

Pt. of Ayre
Cranstal
A10
Andreas
Bride
Sulby
Ramsey Bay
A9
Ballaugh
Ramsey
A3
Maughold
Kirk Michael
16
A14
SNAEFELL
620
A18
Maughold
Hd.
A15
B10
15
Peel
A4
St. John's
B22
Laxey
A27
9
A11
A2
Glenmaye
Onchan
Foxdale
SOUTH
BARRULE
A24
483
A5
9
Douglas
A36
15
A3
A26
A25
HEYSHAM 3:30
Bradda Hd.
Colby
Ballasalla
Port Erin
ISLE OF MAN
Port
St. Mary
Castletown
BELFAST 2:55
DUBLIN 2:55
(April-Sept)
LIVERPOOL 2:30
Calf
of Man
Langness
LARNE 8:00

8   9   10   11   5'00   12   13   14

A

B

REDCAR
Marske-by-the-Sea
Saltburn-by-the-Sea
Skelton   Brotton
A173   RC   Loftus   Staithes
A174
B1366   23   A74   Hinderwell   *Kettle Ness*
Guisborough   Lythe
ton   A171   20   **WHITBY**
51   Sneaton
Egton   Hawsker
Castleton   *Esk*   Sleights   Robin Hood's Bay
ND HILLS
454   Goathland   *Fylingdales*   Staintondale
RTH YORK MOORS   *Moor*   19
NATIONAL PARK   A169   A171   Cloughton
Hodge   Rosedale   Abbey   Burniston
Dove   20   Scalby
Hutton-le-Hole   Lockton   **SCARBOROUGH**
Kirkbymoorside   *Seven*   Ayton   A165
vaulx   A170   Thornton-le-   A165   Eastfield
27   Dale   16   Ebberston   A170   Seamer   B1261
Helmsley   Pickering   Snainton   A64   Filey
Vale of Pickering   B1258   7   *The Carrs*   Sherburn   Staxton   17   Hunmanby   *Filey Bay*
Hovingham   *Rye*   21   B1249   Burton   B1229
B1257   A169   WOLDS   Fleming
HOWARDIAN   Malton   A64   Rillington   A165   Flamborough
Terrington   Norton   Weaverthorpe   B1253   B1255   *Flamborough*
HILLS   I   R   E   Rudston   *Hd.*
llington   Sheriff   B1248   Langtoft   **BRIDLINGTON**
Hutton   19   Acklam   B1253   Kilham   A614   Burton   *Bridlington*
Strensall   Sledmere   13   Agnes   *Bay*
Haxby   A64   Fridaythorpe   Garton-on-   Nafferton   Lissett
New Earswick   A166   the-Wolds   A166   Wetwang   Driffield   46   Skipsea
YORK   Stamford   30   B1249   Beeford   B1242
CITY   Dunnington   Bridge   Bainton   Hutton   North   16   Hornsea
A1079   A1079   19   B1246   Cranswick   Frodingham   A165   B1244
OF   B1228   Elvington   Pocklington   15   **EAST RIDING**   Leven   B1240
YORK   Barmby   A614   Middleton on   **OF**
A19   Wheldrake   Moor   Hayton   the Wolds   **YORKSHIRE**
Escrick   28   Market   6   29   laugh
16   Weighton   B1248   A1035   Aldbrough
call   lme-on-   12   A1079   5'00   erley   12
Spalding-moor   North Newbald

C

D

5'00

E

F

G

H

4'50

J

K

8   9   10   11   12   13   14

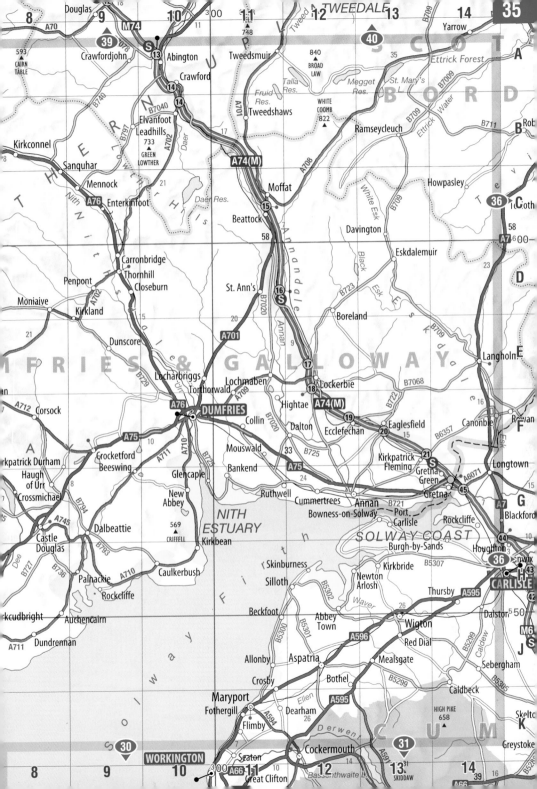

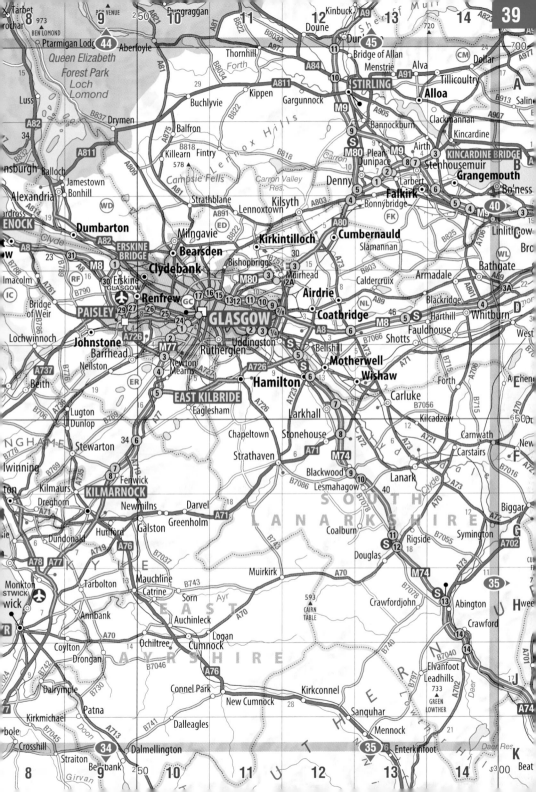

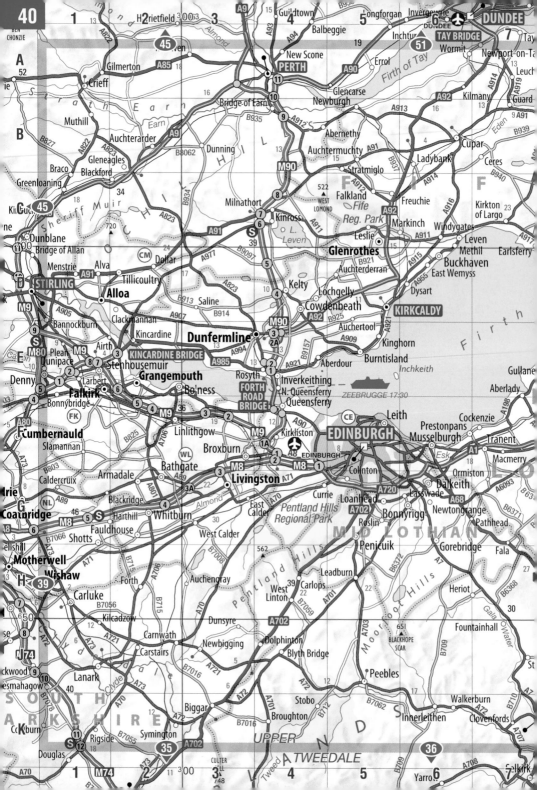

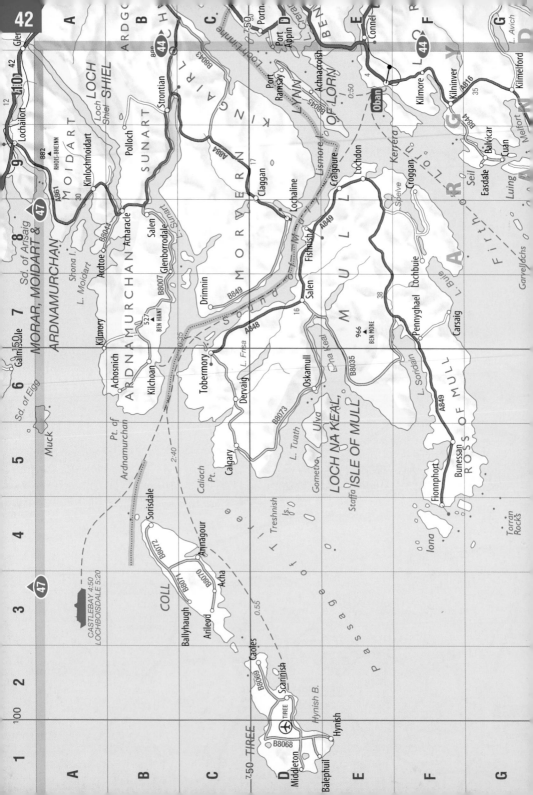

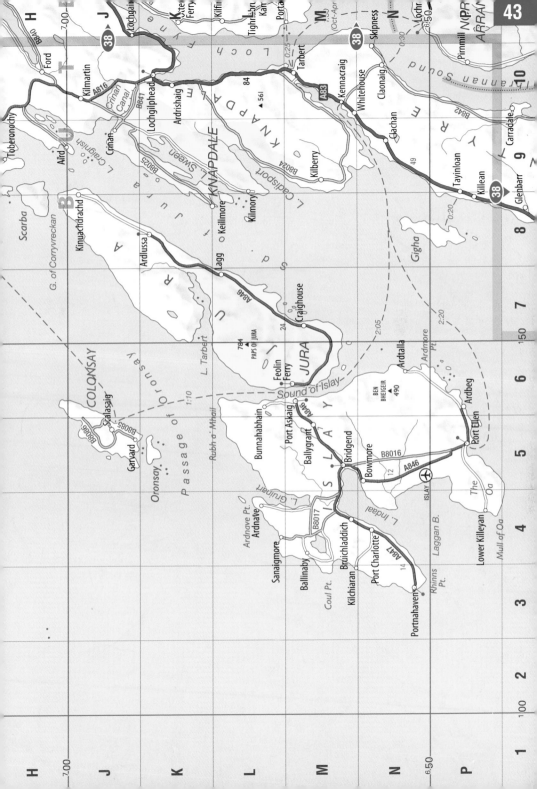

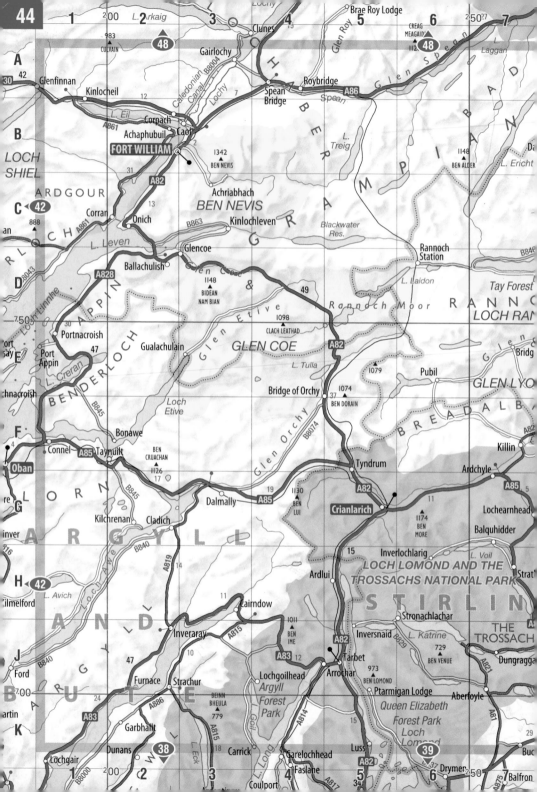

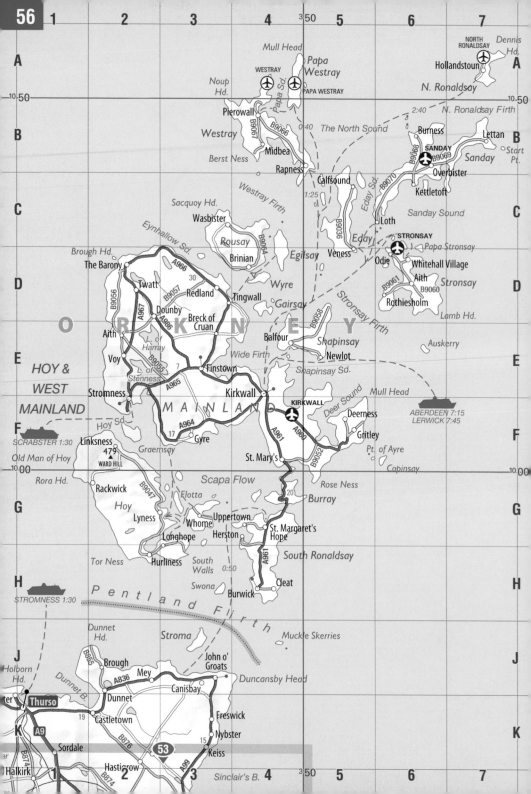

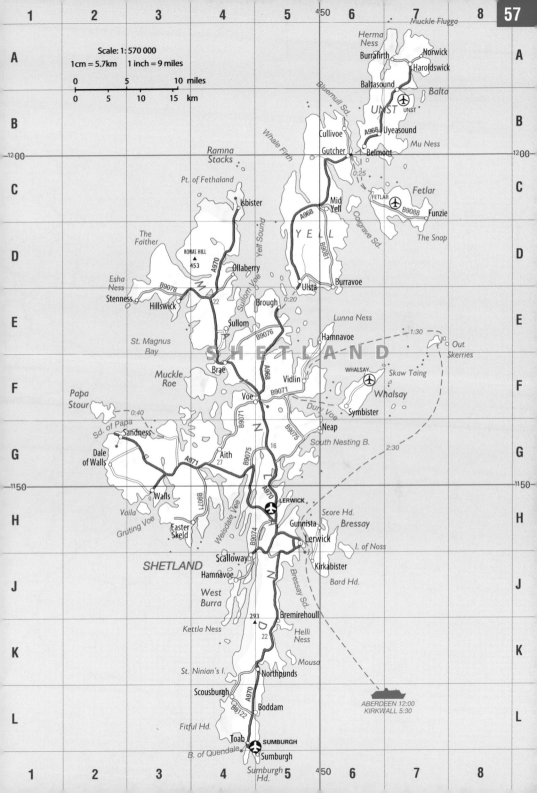

Scale: 1: 570 000

1cm = 5.7km   1 inch = 9 miles

0   5   10 miles

0   5   10   15   km

Muckle Flugga

Herma
Ness
Burrafirth   Norwick
                        Haroldswick
        Baltasound   Balta
            A968   UNST   Balta
        UNST   UNST

Bluemull Sd.

Whale Firth

Cullivoe
Gutcher   Uyeasound
    A968   Belmont   Mu Ness
        0:25

Ramna
Stacks

Pt. of Fethaland   Mid   FETLAR   Fetlar
                        Yell   B9088   Funzie

Isbister   YELL   The Snap

The
Faither   RONAS HILL   A970   Colgrave Sd.
            453   Ollaberry
Esha   B9078   Burravoe
Ness   Hillswick   Ulsta   Lunna Ness
Stenness   0:20
        Hillswick   Brough   Out
            Sullom   Skerries
        St. Magnus   B9076   Hamnavoe   1:30
            Bay
    Muckle   Vidlin   WHALSAY
    Roe   Brae   A968   Skaw Taing
                Voe   B9071   Whalsay
Papa   WHALSAY
Stour   0:40   B9071   Symbister
                    A970   B9075   Neap
    Sd. of Papa   South Nesting B.
Sandness   16   2:30
Dale   A971   Aith   B9075
of Walls   27   Dur   Voe
                        LERWICK
        Walls   B9071   A970   Score Hd.   Bressay
    Vaila   Gunnista
    Gruting Voe   Easter   B9074   Lerwick
            Skeld   Weisdale Voe   I. of Noss
SHETLAND   Scalloway   Kirkabister
        Hamnavoe   Bard Hd.
    West
    Burra   Bressay Sd.
        Kettla Ness   293   Bremirehoull
                    22   Helli
    St. Ninian's I.   Ness   Mousa
            Northpunds
    Scousburgh   A970
        B9122   Boddam   ABERDEEN 12:00
    Fitful Hd.   KIRKWALL 5:30
            Toab   SUMBURGH
    B. of Quendale   Sumburgh
        Sumburgh
        Hd.

1200   1200

1150   1150

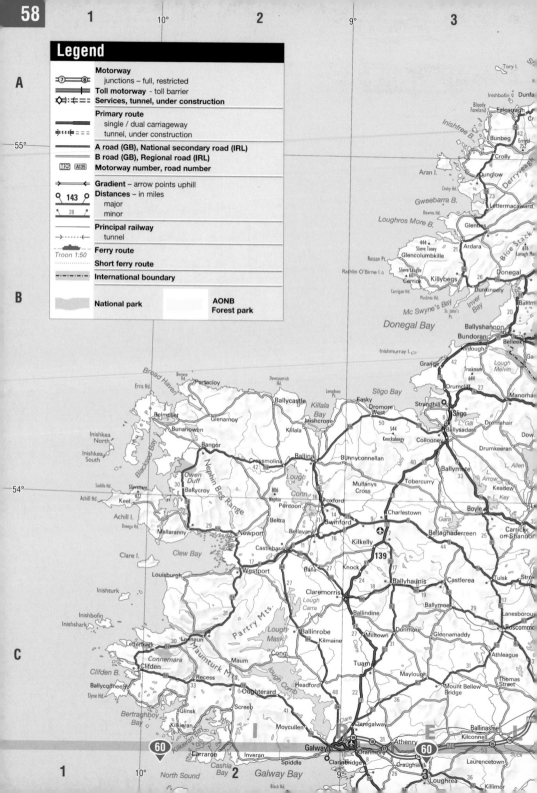

Index to road maps of Ireland

A

Abbey 60 A3
Abbeydorney.....60 B2
Abbeyfeale.......60 B2
Abbeyleix 61 B4
Adare 60 B3
Adrigole 60 C2
Aghalee 59 B5
Ahoghill 59 B5
Allihies 60 C1
Anascaul 60 B1
Annalong 59 B6
Annestown.......61 B4
Antrim............59 B5
Ardagh 60 B2
Ardara...........58 B3
Ardee 59 C5
Ardfert 60 B2
Ardglass 59 B6
Ardgroom........60 C2
Ardkearagh 60 C1
Arklow 61 B5
Armagh..........59 B5
Armoy 59 A5
Arthurstown 61 B5
Ashbourne.......59 C5
Askeaton 60 B3
Athboy 59 C5
Athea............60 B2
Athenry..........60 A3
Athleague 58 C3
Athlone..........61 A4
Athy.............61 B5
Augher 59 B4
Aughnacloy......59 B5
Aughrim.........61 B5

B

Bailieborough......59 C5
Balbriggan........59 C5
Balla 58 C2
Ballaghaderreen 58 C3
Ballina...........58 B2
Ballinalack.......59 C4
Ballinamore......59 B4
Ballinascarty.....60 C3
Ballinasloe.......60 A3
Ballindine........58 C3
Ballingarry
  Limerick........60 B3
  Tipperary 61 B4
Ballingeary.......60 C2
Ballinhassig......60 C3
Ballinrobe.......58 C2
Ballinskelligs....60 C1
Ballinspittle......60 C3
Ballintra.........58 B3
Ballivor.........59 C5
Ballon...........61 B5
Ballybay.........59 B5
Ballybofey.......59 B4
Ballybunion......60 B2
Ballycanew 61 B5
Ballycarry.......59 B6
Ballycastle
  Antrim........59 A5
  Mayo.........58 B2
Ballyclare.......59 B6
Ballyconneely....58 C1
Ballycotton 60 C3

Ballycroy 58 B2
Ballydehob........60 C2
Ballyferriter.......60 B1
Ballygawley.......59 B4
Ballygowan 59 B6
Ballyhaunis.......58 C3
Ballyheige........60 B2
Ballyjamesduff ...59 C4
Ballylanders......60 B3
Ballylynan 61 B4
Ballymahon 59 C4
Ballymena 59 B5
Ballymoe 58 C3
Ballymoney......59 A5
Ballymore 59 C4
Ballymote........58 B3
Ballynacorra......60 C3
Ballynagore.......61 A4
Ballynahinch......59 B6
Ballynure 59 B6
Ballyragget 61 B4
Ballysadare......58 B3
Ballyshannon 58 B3
Ballyvaghan......60 A2
Ballyvourney 60 C2
Ballywalter 59 B6
Baltimore........60 C2
Baltinglass.......61 B5
Banbridge........59 B5
Bandon..........60 C3
Bangor
  Down 59 B6
  Mayo 58 B2
Banteer..........60 B3
Bantry...........60 C2
Beaufort.........60 B2
Belcoo...........59 B4
Belfast 59 B6
Belgooly.........60 C3
Bellananagh 59 C4
Bellavary........58 C2
Belleek 58 B3
Belmullet........58 B2
Beltra 58 C2
Belturbet 59 B4
Beragh 59 B4
Birr 61 A4
Blackwater 61 B5
Blarney 60 C3
Blessington......61 A5
Borris 61 B5
Borris-in-Ossory....61 B4
Borrisokane......60 B3
Borrisoleigh 61 B4
Boyle...........58 C3
Bracklin 59 C5
Bray............61 A5
Broadford........60 B3
Broughshane.....59 B5
Bruff 60 B3
Bunahowen......58 B2
Bunbeg.........58 A3
Bunclody 61 B5
Buncrana 59 A4
Bundoran........58 B3
Bunmahon 61 B4
Bunnyconnellan 58 B2
Bunratty.........60 B3
Bushmills........59 A5
Butler's Bridge...59 B4
Buttevant 60 B3

C

Caher 61 B4
Caherciveen......60 C1
Caherdaniel......60 C1
Caledon 59 B5
Callan 61 B4
Camp............60 B2
Cappamore 60 B3
Cappoquin 61 B4
Carlingford 59 B5
Carlow 61 B5
Carndonagh 59 A4
Carnew...........61 B5
Carnlough 59 B6
Carraroe.........60 A2
Carrick 58 B3
Carrickart 59 A4
Carrickfergus 59 B6
Carrickmacross ...59 C5
Carrick-on-
  Shannon 58 C3
Carrick-on-Suir....61 B4
Carrigallen 59 C4
Carryduff 59 B6
Cashel 61 B4
Castlebar 58 C2
Castlebellingham...59 C5
Castlebridge......61 B5
Castleblaney 59 B5
Castlecomer 61 B4
Castlederg 59 B4
Castledermot 61 B5
Castleisland......60 B2
Castlemaine 60 B2
Castlemartyr.....60 C3
Castlepollard.....59 C4
Castlerea 58 C3
Castletown
  Bearhaven....60 C2
Castletownroche ..60 B3
Castlewellan 59 B6
Cavan...........59 C4
Celbridge........61 A5
Charlestown.....58 C3
Charleville.......60 B3
Clarecastle 60 B3
Claregalway......60 A3
Claremorris......58 C3
Clarinbridge......60 A3
Clashmore.......61 B4
Claudy..........59 B4
Clifden..........58 C1
Clogh............61 B4
Cloghan
  Donegal 59 B4
  Offaly 61 A4
Clogheen 61 B4
Clogher..........59 B4
Cloghjordan......60 B3
Clonakilty.......60 C3
Clonaslee........61 A4
Clondalkin.......61 A5
Clones 59 B4
Clonmany........59 A4
Clonmel 61 B4
Clonmellon......59 C4
Clonord..........59 C4
Clonroche 61 B5
Cloone 59 C4
Clough 59 B6
Cloyne..........60 C3
Coachford 60 C3

Coagh 59 B5
Coalisland.......59 B5
Cóbh............60 C3
Coleraine........59 A5
Collon 59 C5
Collooney........58 B3
Comber..........59 B6
Cong 58 C2
Conna 60 B3
Connaugh 60 B3
Cookstown......59 B5
Coolgreany 61 B5
Cooneen 59 B4
Cootehill 59 B4
Cork............60 C3
Craughwell 60 A3
Creeslough 59 A4
Creeve..........59 B5
Crolly...........58 A3
Crookhaven......60 C2
Crookstown......60 C3
Croom..........60 B3
Crossakiel 59 C4
Crosshaven......60 C3
Crossmolina.....58 B2
Crumlin 59 B5
Crusheen 60 B3
Cullaville 59 B5
Cushendall.......59 A5

D

Daingean 61 A4
Dalkey 61 A5
Darragh.........60 B2
Delvin 59 C4
Derrygonnelly....59 B4
Derrylin.........59 B4
Derry/Londonderry..59 A5
Dervock.........59 A5
Dingle 60 B1
Donaghadee.....59 B6
Donegal 58 B3
Doonbeg.........60 B2
Downhill.........59 A5
Downpatrick.....59 B6
Dowra 58 B3
Draperstown.....59 B5
Drimoleague.....60 C2
Drogheda........59 C5
Dromahair.......58 B3
Dromcolliher.....60 B3
Dromore
  Down 59 B5
  Tyrone 59 B4
Dromore West....58 B3
Drumcliff........58 B3
Drumkeeran 58 B3
Drumquin........59 B4
Drumshanbo.....58 B3
Drumsna.........59 C4
Dublin 61 A5
Duleek 59 C5
Dunboyne.......61 A5
Dundalk 59 B5
Dundrum 59 B6
Dunfanaghy......59 A4
Dungannon......59 B5
Dungarvan.......61 B4
Dungiven 59 B5
Dunglow.........58 B3
Dungourney 60 C3
Dunkineely......58 B3

Dun Laoghaire 61 A5
Dunlavin.........61 A5
Dunleer 59 C5
Dunloy 59 A5
Dunmanway 60 C2
Dunmore.........58 C3
Dunmore East....61 B5
Dunmurry.......59 B5
Dunshaughlin....59 C5
Durrow 61 B4
Durrus 60 C2

E

Easky...........58 B3
Edenderry.......61 A4
Edgeworthstown....59 C4
Eglinton 59 A4
Emyvale 59 B5
Enfield 59 C5
Ennis 60 B3
Enniscorthy......61 B5
Enniskean 60 C3
Enniskillen.......59 B4
Ennistimon 60 B2

F

Falcarragh.......58 A3
Farranfore.......60 B2
Feeny 59 B4
Fenagh 59 B4
Fenit 60 B2
Ferbane 61 A4
Fermoy 60 B3
Ferns 61 B5
Fethard
  Tipperary 61 B4
  Wexford 61 B5
Finnea..........59 C4
Fintona 59 B4
Fivemiletown 59 B4
Fontstown 61 A5
Foxford 58 C2
Foynes 60 B2
Freshford........61 B4

G

Galway 60 A2
Garrison.........58 B3
Garvagh 59 B5
Gilford...........59 B5
Glenamoy........58 B2
Glenarm 59 B6
Glenavy 59 B5
Glenbeigh 60 B2
Glencolumbkille...58 B3
Glendalough 61 A5
Glenealy.........61 B5
Glengarriff.......60 C2
Glennamaddy....58 C3
Glenties 58 B3
Glin 60 B2
Glinsk 60 A2
Gorey...........61 B5
Gort 60 A3
Gortin 59 B4
Gowran..........61 B4
Graiguenamanagh...61 B5
Granard 59 C4

Grange 58 B3
Greenisland 59 B6
Greystones 61 A5

H

Hacketstown 61 B5
Headford 58 C2
Herbertstown 60 B3
Hillsborough 59 B5
Holycross 61 B4
Holywood 59 B6
Hospital 60 B3

I

Inagh 60 B2
Inishannon 60 C3
Inishcrone 58 B2
Inveran 60 A2
Irvinestown 59 B4

J

Johnstown 61 B4
Julianstown 59 C5

K

Kanturk 60 B3
Keadew 58 B3
Keady 59 B5
Keel 58 C1
Keenagh 59 C4
Kells
  Antrim 59 B5
  Meath 59 C5
Kenmare 60 C2
Kesh 59 B4
Kilbaha 60 B2
Kilbeggan 61 A4
Kilcock 59 C5
Kilconnell 60 A3
Kilcormac 61 A4
Kilcullen 61 A5
Kilcurry 59 B5
Kildare 61 A5
Kildorrery 60 B3
Kilgarvan 60 C2
Kilkee 60 B2
Kilkeel 59 B5
Kilkelly 58 C3
Kilkenny 61 B4
Kilkieran 60 A2
Kilkinlea 60 B2
Killadysert 60 B2
Killala 58 B2
Killaloe 60 B3
Killarney 60 B2
Killashandra 59 B4
Killashee 59 C4
Killeigh 61 A4
Killenaule 61 B4
Killimor 60 A3
Killinaboy 60 B2
Killinick 61 B5
Killorglin 60 B2
Killucan 59 C4
Killybegs 58 B3
Killyleagh 59 B6

Kilmacrenan 59 A4
Kilmacthomas 61 B4
Kilmaine 58 C2
Kilmallock 60 B3
Kilmeadan 61 B4
Kilmeedy 60 B3
Kilmore Quay 61 B5
Kilnaleck 59 C4
Kilrea 59 B5
Kilrush 60 B2
Kiltoom 58 C3
Kingarrow 58 B3
Kingscourt 59 C5
Kinlough 58 B3
Kinnegad 59 C4
Kinnitty 61 A4
Kinsale 60 C3
Kinvarra 60 A3
Kircubbin 59 B6
Knock 58 C3
Knocktopher 61 B4

L

Laban 60 A3
Lanesborough 59 C4
Laragh 61 A5
Larne 59 B6
Lauragh 60 C2
Laurencetown 60 A3
Leap 60 C2
Leenaun 58 C2
Leighlinbridge 61 B5
Leitrim 58 C3
Letterfrack 58 C2
Letterkenny 59 B4
Lettermacaward 58 B3
Lifford 59 B4
Limavady 59 A5
Limerick 60 B3
Lisbellaw 59 B4
Lisburn 59 B5
Liscannor 60 B2
Lisdoonvarna 60 A2
Lismore 61 B4
Lisnaskea 59 B4
Lissycasey 60 B2
Listowel 60 B2
Littleton 61 B4
Longford 59 C4
Loughbrickland 59 B5
Loughrea 60 A3
Louisburgh 58 C2
Lucan 61 A5
Lurgan 59 B5

M

Macroom 60 C3
Maghera 59 B5
Magherafelt 59 B5
Maguiresbridge 59 B4
Malahide 59 C5
Malin 59 A4
Mallaranny 58 C2
Mallow 60 B3
Manorhamilton 58 B3
Markethill 59 B5
Maum 58 C2
Maylough 58 C3
Middletown 59 B5
Midleton 60 C3

Milford 59 A4
Millstreet
  Cork 60 B2
  Waterford 61 B4
Milltown
  Galway 58 C3
  Kerry 60 B1
Milltown Malbay 60 B2
Mitchelstown 60 B3
Moate 61 A4
Mohill 59 C4
Monaghan 59 B5
Monasterevin 61 A4
Moneygall 61 B4
Moneymore 59 B5
Mount Bellew
  Bridge 58 C3
Mountfield 59 B4
Mountmellick 61 A4
Mountrath 61 B4
Moville 59 A4
Moy 59 B5
Moycullen 60 A2
Muckross 60 B2
Muff 59 A4
Muine Bheag 61 B5
Mullanys Cross 58 B3
Mullinavat 61 B4
Mullingar 59 C4

N

Naas 61 A5
Naul 59 C5
Navan 59 C5
Nenagh 60 B3
Newbliss 59 B4
Newbridge 61 A5
Newcastle 59 B6
Newcastle West 60 B2
Newinn 61 B4
Newmarket 60 B3
Newmarket-on-
  Fergus 60 B3
Newport
  Mayo 58 C2
  Tipperary 60 B3
New Ross 61 B5
Newry 59 B5
Newtownabbey 59 B6
Newtownards 59 B6
Newtownbutler 59 B4
Newtown
  Cunningham 59 B4
Newtown Hamilton . . 59 B5
Newtownmount-
  kennedy 61 A5
Newtown Sands 60 B2
Newtownstewart 59 B4
Ninemilehouse 61 B4

O

Oilgate 61 B5
Oldcastle 59 C4
Omagh 59 B4
Oranmore 60 A3
Oughterard 58 C2

P

Pallas Green 60 B3
Parknasilla 60 C2
Passage East 61 B5
Patrickswell 60 B3
Paulstown 61 B4
Peterswell 60 A3
Pettigo 59 B4
Plumbridge 59 B4
Pomeroy 59 B5
Pontoon 58 C2
Portacloy 58 B2
Portadown 59 B5
Portaferry 59 B6
Portarlington 61 A4
Portavogie 59 B6
Portglenone 59 B5
Portlaoise 61 A4
Portmagne 60 C1
Portroe 60 B3
Portrush 59 A5
Portstewart 59 A5
Portumna 60 A3
Poyntz Pass 59 B5

R

Randalstown 59 B5
Rathangan 61 A5
Rathcoole 61 A5
Rathcormack 60 B3
Rathdrum 61 B5
Rathfriland 59 B5
Rathkeale 60 B3
Rathmelton 59 A4
Rathmolyon 59 C5
Rathmore 60 B2
Rathmullan 59 A4
Rathnew 61 B5
Rathvilly 61 B5
Recess 58 C2
Ringaskiddy 60 C3
Roosky 59 C4
Roscommon 58 C3
Roscrea 61 B4
Rosslare 61 B5
Rosslare Harbour 61 B5
Rosslea 59 B4
Roundwood 61 A5
Rush 59 C5

S

Saintfield 59 B6
Sallins 61 A5
Scarriff 60 B3
Screeb 60 A2
Seskinore 59 B4
Shanagolden 60 B2
Shercock 59 C5
Shillelagh 61 B5
Silvermines 60 B3
Sion Mills 59 B4
Skerries 59 C5
Skibbereen 60 C2
Slane 59 C5
Sligo 58 B3
Sneem 60 C2
Spiddle 60 A2
St Johnstown 59 B4

Strabane 59 B4
Stradbally 60 B1
Strandhill 58 B3
Strangford 59 B6
Stranorlar 59 B4
Strokestown 58 C3
Swanlinbar 59 B4
Swatragh 59 B5
Swinford 58 C3
Swords 59 C5

T

Tallaght 61 A5
Tallow 60 B3
Tarbert 60 B2
Templederry 60 B3
Templemore 61 B4
Termonfeckin 59 C5
Thomas Street 58 C3
Thomastown 61 B4
Thurles 61 B4
Timoleague 60 C3
Timolin 61 B5
Tipperary 60 B3
Tobercurry 58 B3
Tobermore 59 B5
Toomyvara 60 B3
Toormore 60 C2
Tralee 60 B2
Tramore 61 B4
Trim 59 C5
Tuam 58 C3
Tulla 60 B3
Tullamore 61 A4
Tullow 61 B5
Tulsk 58 C3
Tyrrellspass 61 A4

U

Urlingford 61 B4

V

Virginia 59 C4

W

Warrenpoint 59 B5
Waterford 61 B4
Watergrasshill 60 B3
Waterville 60 C1
Wellingtonbridge 61 B5
Westport 58 C2
Wexford 61 B5
Whitegate 60 C3
Whitehead 59 B6
Wicklow 61 B5

Y

Youghal 61 C4

Index to road maps of Great Britain

How to use the index

Example

Gillingham Dorset **5 A11**

grid square

page number

county or unitary authority (only shown for duplicate names)

Abbreviations used in the index

Aberdeen **Aberdeen City**	Glasgow **City of Glasgow**	Poole **Poole**
Aberds **Aberdeenshire**	Glos **Gloucestershire**	Powys **Powys**
Ald **Alderney**	Gtr Man **Greater Manchester**	Ptsmth **Portsmouth**
Anglesey **Isle of Anglesey**	Guern **Guernsey**	Reading **Reading**
Angus **Angus**	Gwyn **Gwynedd**	Redcar **Redcar and Cleveland**
Argyll **Argyll and Bute**	Halton **Halton**	Renfs **Renfrewshire**
Bath **Bath and North East Somerset**	Hants **Hampshire**	Rhondda **Rhondda Cynon Taff**
Bedford **Bedford**	Hereford **Herefordshire**	Rutland **Rutland**
Bl Gwent **Blaenau Gwent**	Herts **Hertfordshire**	S Ayrs **South Ayrshire**
Blackburn **Blackburn with Darwen**	Highld **Highland**	S Glos **South Gloucestershire**
Blackpool **Blackpool**	Hrtlpl **Hartlepool**	S Lanark **South Lanarkshire**
Bmouth **Bournemouth**	Hull **Hull**	S Yorks **South Yorkshire**
Borders **Scottish Borders**	IoM **Isle of Man**	Scilly **Scilly**
Brack **Bracknell**	IoW **Isle of Wight**	Shetland **Shetland**
Bridgend **Bridgend**	Invclyd **Inverclyde**	Shrops **Shropshire**
Brighton **City of Brighton and Hove**	Jersey **Jersey**	Slough **Slough**
Bristol **City and County of Bristol**	Kent **Kent**	Som **Somerset**
Bucks **Buckinghamshire**	Lancs **Lancashire**	Soton **Southampton**
C Beds **Central Bedfordshire**	Leicester **City of Leicester**	Southend **Southend-on-Sea**
Caerph **Caerphilly**	Leics **Leicestershire**	Staffs **Staffordshire**
Cardiff **Cardiff**	Lincs **Lincolnshire**	Stirling **Stirling**
Carms **Carmarthenshire**	London **Greater London**	Stockton **Stockton-on-Tees**
Ceredig **Ceredigion**	Luton **Luton**	Stoke **Stoke-on-Trent**
Ches E **Cheshire East**	M Keynes **Milton Keynes**	Suff **Suffolk**
Ches W **Cheshire West and Chester**	M Tydf **Merthyr Tydfil**	Sur **Surrey**
Clack **Clackmannanshire**	Mbro **Middlesbrough**	Swansea **Swansea**
Conwy **Conwy**	Medway **Medway**	Swindon **Swindon**
Corn **Cornwall**	Mers **Merseyside**	T&W **Tyne and Wear**
Cumb **Cumbria**	Midloth **Midlothian**	Telford **Telford and Wrekin**
Darl **Darlington**	Mon **Monmouthshire**	Thurrock **Thurrock**
Denb **Denbighshire**	Moray **Moray**	Torbay **Torbay**
Derby **City of Derby**	N Ayrs **North Ayrshire**	Torf **Torfaen**
Derbys **Derbyshire**	N Lincs **North Lincolnshire**	V Glam **The Vale of Glamorgan**
Devon **Devon**	N Lanark **North Lanarkshire**	W Berks **West Berkshire**
Dorset **Dorset**	N Som **North Somerset**	W Dunb **West Dunbartonshire**
Dumfries **Dumfries and Galloway**	N Yorks **North Yorkshire**	W Isles **Western Isles**
Dundee **Dundee City**	NE Lincs **North East Lincolnshire**	W Loth **West Lothian**
Durham **Durham**	Neath **Neath Port Talbot**	W Mid **West Midlands**
E Ayrs **East Ayrshire**	Newport **City and County of Newport**	W Sus **West Sussex**
E Dunb **East Dunbartonshire**	Norf **Norfolk**	W Yorks **West Yorkshire**
E Loth **East Lothian**	Northants **Northamptonshire**	Warks **Warwickshire**
E Renf **East Renfrewshire**	Northumb **Northumberland**	Warr **Warrington**
E Sus **East Sussex**	Nottingham **City of Nottingham**	Wilts **Wiltshire**
E Yorks **East Riding of Yorkshire**	Notts **Nottinghamshire**	Windsor **Windsor and Maidenhead**
Edin **City of Edinburgh**	Orkney **Orkney**	Wokingham **Wokingham**
Essex **Essex**	Oxon **Oxfordshire**	Worcs **Worcestershire**
Falk **Falkirk**	Pboro **Peterborough**	Wrex **Wrexham**
Fife **Fife**	Pembs **Pembrokeshire**	York **City of York**
Flint **Flintshire**	Perth **Perth and Kinross**	
	Plym **Plymouth**	

A

Abbey Town 35 H12
Abbots Bromley 21 D11
Abbotsbury 5 E9
Aberaeron 19 P4
Aberarth 19 P4
Abercarn 7 B11
Aberchirder 50 B5
Abercraf 13 E12
Aberdare 13 F13
Aberdaron 18 H1
Aberdeen 50 G8
Aberdour 40 E4
Aberdulais 13 G11
Aberdyfi 19 L6
Aberfeldy 45 E10
Aberffraw 18 D3
Aberfoyle 44 J7
Abergavenny 14 E1
Abergele 18 C9
Abergwili 12 D8
Abergwyngregyn ... 18 C6
Abergynolwyn 19 K6
Aberlady 40 E7
Abernethy 40 B4
Aberporth 12 A6
Abersoch 18 H3
Abersychan 7 A11
Abertillery 7 A11
Aberystwyth 19 M5
Abingdon 15 G14
Abington 35 A10
Aboyne 51 H4
Accrington 27 C8
Acha 42 C3
Achanalt 48 B3
Achaphubuil 44 B2
Acharacle 42 B8
Achavanich 53 D13
Achiemore 52 B5
Achiltibuie 52 H2
Achnacroish 42 D10
Achnasheen 48 C2
Achnashellach 46 G10
Achosnich 42 B6
Achriabhach 44 C3
Acklam 33 H9
Acle 24 D8
Acomb 32 J7
Acton Burnell 20 F6
Addingham 32 J2
Adlington 26 D7
Adwick le Street... 28 D4
Affric Lodge 48 F2
Ainsdale 26 D4
Aird 43 H9
Aird a Mhulaidh .. 55 F3
Aird Asaig Tairbeart /
   Tarbert 55 G3
Airdrie 39 D12
Aird Uig 55 D2
Airor 47 L7
Airth 39 B14
Aisgill 31 E13
Aith
   Orkney 56 D6
   Orkney 56 E2
   Shetland 57 G4
Akeley 16 B2
Albrighton 21 F9
Alcester 15 A9
Aldborough 32 H6
Aldbourne 15 J11
Aldbrough 29 A11
Aldeburgh 25 K9
Alderbury 8 E6
Alderley Edge 27 H9
Aldermaston 9 A10
Aldershot 9 B13
Aldridge 21 F11
Aldsworth 15 E10
Aldwick 9 H14
Alexandria 39 B8
Alford
   Aberds 50 F4
   Lincs 29 G13
Alfreton 28 J3

Alfriston 10 J6
Alkham 11 E13
Allendale Town 36 H7
Allenheads 36 J7
Alloa 39 A13
Allonby 35 J11
Alltforgan 18 H9
Almondsbury 14 H5
Alness 48 B7
Alnmouth 37 B11
Alnwick 37 B10
Alphington 4 E3
Alrewas 21 E12
Alsager 21 A9
Alston 36 J6
Altanduino 53 F10
Altarnun 3 D10
Altass 52 H7
Althorne 17 F14
Althorpe 28 C7
Altnabreac Station .53 D12
Alt na h'Airbhe .. 52 J3
Altnaharra 52 E7
Alton
   Hants 9 D12
   Staffs 21 B11
Altrincham 27 G8
Alva 39 A13
Alvechurch 21 J11
Alveley 21 H8
Alveston 14 H5
Alvie 49 H9
Alwinton 37 C8
Alyth 51 N1
Amble 37 C11
Ambleside 31 D9
Ambrosden 16 D1
Amersham 16 F4
Amesbury 8 C6
Amlwch 18 A4
Ammanford 13 E10
Ampleforth 32 G7
Ampthill 16 B5
Amulree 45 F11
Ancaster 23 A8
Ancroft 41 J12
Ancrum 36 A5
Andover 9 C8
Andoversford ... 15 E9
Andreas 30 E4
Angle 12 F2
Angmering 10 J1
Annan 35 G12
Annbank 34 A5
Annfield Plain .. 37 H10
Anstey 22 E4
Anstruther 41 C8
An t-Ob /
   Leverburgh ... 55 J2
Appleby-in-
   Westmorland ..31 B12
Applecross 46 G7
Appledore
   Devon 6 J3
   Kent 11 G10
Arbroath 51 N5
Archiestown 49 D13
Ardarroch 46 G8
Ardbeg 43 P6
Ardcharnich 52 K3
Ardchyle 44 G7
Ardentinny 38 B6
Ardersier 49 C8
Ardessie 52 K2
Ardgay 52 J7
Ardhasig 55 G3
Ardingly 10 G4
Ardlamont Ho. .. 38 D4
Ardleigh 25 N5
Ardley 15 D14
Ardlui 44 H5
Ardlussa 43 K8
Ardminish 43 L4
Ardrishaig 38 B3
Ardrossan 38 F7
Ardtalla 43 N6
Ardtalnaig 45 F9
Ardtoe 42 A8
Ardvasar 47 L6

Ardwell
   Dumfries 34 J2
   Moray 50 E2
Arileod 42 C3
Arinagour 42 C4
Arisaig 47 N6
Armadale
   Highland 47 L6
   W Loth 40 G2
Armathwaite 36 J4
Armitage 21 E11
Armscote 28 D5
Arncliffe 32 G1
Arncott 16 D1
Arnisdale 47 K8
Arnold 22 A4
Arnside 31 G10
Arreton 9 J10
Arrochar 44 J5
Arundel 10 J1
Ascot 16 J4
Asfordby 22 C6
Ash
   Kent 11 D13
   Sur 9 C13
Ashbourne 21 B12
Ashburton 4 G1
Ashbury 15 H11
Ashby de-la-Zouch .22 D2
Ashchurch 15 C8
Ashford
   Derbys 27 J12
   Kent 11 E11
Ashingdon 17 F13
Ashington 37 E11
Ashley 21 C8
Ashton 26 J5
Ashton-in-
   Makerfield ... 26 F6
Ashton Keynes .. 15 G9
Ashton under Hill... 15 C9
Ashton under Lyne .27 F10
Ashurst 9 G8
Ashwater 3 B11
Ashwell 16 B7
Ashwick 8 C1
Askam-in-Furness .31 G8
Askern 28 C4
Askrigg 32 E1
Aspatria 35 J12
Astwood Bank .. 21 K11
Atherstone 22 F2
Atherton 26 E7
Attleborough .. 24 F5
Atworth 8 A3
Auchduart 52 H2
Auchenblae ... 51 J6
Auchenbreck .. 38 B5
Auchencairn ... 35 H8
Auchengray ... 40 H3
Auchertool 40 D5
Auchinleck 34 A6
Auchronie 51 J3
Auchterarder .. 45 H11
Auchterderran . 40 D5
Auchtermuchty . 40 B5
Auchtertyre ... 47 J8
Audlem 20 B7
Audley 21 A8
Auldearn 49 C10
Aultbea 46 C8
Austwick 31 H13
Avebury 15 K10
Aveton Gifford . 3 G14
Aviemore 49 G9
Avoch 48 C8
Avonmouth 14 J4
Axbridge 7 F13
Axminster 4 D6
Axmouth 4 E6
Aylesbury 16 D3
Aylesford 11 D8
Aylesham 11 D13
Aylsham 24 C6
Aynho 15 C14
Ayr 34 A4
Aysgarth 32 F5
Ayton
   Borders 41 G12

Ayton *continued*
   N Yorks 33 F11

B

Bac 55 C6
Backwell 7 E13
Bacton 24 B8
Badenscoth 50 D6
Badenyon 50 F2
Badminton 14 H7
Badrallach 52 J2
Bagh a Chaisteil /
   Castlebay 54 K3
Bagillt 26 H3
Bagshot 16 J4
Baildon 27 B12
Baile 54 A6
Baile Ailein 55 E5
Baile Mhartainn . 54 B4
Bainbridge 32 E1
Bainton 33 J11
Bakewell 27 J13
Bala 18 G9
Balbeggie 45 F13
Balblair 49 B8
Balcombe 10 G4
Balderton 28 J7
Baldock 16 B7
Balephuil 42 D1
Balfour 56 E4
Balfron 39 B10
Balintore 49 A9
Ballachulish ... 44 D2
Ballantrae 34 E2
Ballasalla 30 H2
Ballater 51 H2
Ballaugh 30 F3
Ballinaby 43 M4
Ballinluig 45 D11
Balloch
   Highland 49 D8
   W Dunb 39 B8
Ballochan 51 H4
Ballygrant 43 M5
Ballyhaugh 42 C3
Balmacara 47 J8
Balmaclellan .. 34 F7
Balmedie 50 F8
Balnacoil 53 H10
Balnapaling ... 49 B8
Balquhidder ... 44 G7
Balsall 21 J13
Balsham 23 K14
Baltasound 57 A7
Balvicar 42 G9
Bamber Bridge .26 C6
Bamburgh 41 K14
Bamford 27 G13
Bampton
   Devon 4 A3
   Oxon 15 F12
Banbury 15 C13
Banchory 51 H5
Banff 50 A5
Bangor 18 C5
Bangor-is-y-coed .20 B5
Banham 24 G5
Bankend 35 G11
Bankfoot 45 F12
Bankhead 50 F7
Banks 26 C4
Bannockburn .. 39 A13
Banstead 10 D3
Banwell 7 F12
Barabhas 55 B5
Barassie 39 G8
Barbon 31 F12
Bardney 29 H10
Bardsey 22 J1
Bargoed 7 B10
Bargrennan ... 34 F4
Barham 11 E13
Bar Hill 23 J12
Barkway 17 B8
Barlborough .. 28 G3
Barlby 28 A5
Barley 17 B9

Barmby Moor ... 33 K9
Barmoor Castle .. 41 J12
Barmouth 19 J6
Barnard Castle .. 32 C2
Barnet 16 F7
Barnetby le Wold .. 29 D9
Barnham 24 H3
Barnhill 49 C12
Barnoldswick .. 27 A9
Barnsley 28 D2
Barnstaple 6 H4
Barnt Green ... 21 J11
Barr 34 D3
Barrhead 39 E9
Barrhill 34 E3
Barrowford 27 B9
Barrow-in-Furness .30 G7
Barrow upon
   Humber 29 B9
Barry
   Angus 51 P4
   V Glam 7 E10
Barton 32 D4
Barton-le-Clay .. 16 C5
Barton upon
   Humber 29 B9
Barwell 22 F3
Baschurch 20 D5
Basildon 17 G12
Basingstoke 9 B11
Baslow 27 H13
Baston 23 D10
Bath 8 A2
Bathford 8 A2
Bathgate 40 G2
Batley 27 C13
Battle 11 H8
Bawdeswell ... 24 C5
Bawdsey 25 L8
Bawtry 28 E5
Bayston Hill .. 20 F5
Beachley 14 G4
Beaconsfield .. 16 G4
Beadnell 37 A11
Beaminster ... 5 D8
Bearsden 39 C10
Bearsted 11 D8
Beattock 35 C11
Beaufort 13 E15
Beaulieu 9 G8
Beauly 48 D6
Beaumaris 18 C5
Bebington ... 26 G4
Beccles 24 F9
Beckermet ... 30 D6
Beckfoot 35 J11
Beckhampton .15 K10
Beckingham .. 28 E6
Beckington .. 8 B3
Beck Row 24 H1
Bedale 32 F4
Beddgelert .. 18 F5
Bedford 16 A5
Bedlington .. 37 E11
Bedwas 7 C10
Bedworth 22 G2
Beeford 33 J13
Beer 4 E6
Beeston 22 B4
Beeswing 35 G9
Beetley 12 F5
Beguildy 20 J3
Beighton 28 F3
Beith 39 E8
Belbroughton . 21 J10
Belchford 29 G11
Belford 41 K14
Bellingham .. 36 F7
Bellsbank ... 34 C5
Bellshill 39 D12
Belmont
   Blackburn 26 D7
   Shetland 57 B6
Belper 28 K2
Belsay 37 F9
Beltingham .. 11 C12

Belton
N Lincs 28 D6
Norf 24 E9
Bembridge 9 J11
Benington 23 A12
Benllech 18 B5
Benson 16 F1
Bentley
Hants 9 C12
S Yorks 28 D4
Benwick 23 F12
Bere Alston 3 E12
Bere Regis 8 H3
Berkeley 14 G5
Berkhamsted 16 E4
Berriedale 53 F13
Berriew 20 F2
Berrow 7 F11
Berwick 10 J6
Berwick-upon-
Tweed 41 H12
Bethersden 11 F10
Bethesda 18 D6
Bettws Bledrws 19 Q6
Bettyhill 53 B9
Betws 13 H13
Betws-y-Coed 18 E7
Beulah 13 A13
Beverley 29 A9
Bewcastle 36 F4
Bewdley 21 J8
Bexhill 11 J8
Bexley 10 B5
Bibury 15 F10
Bicester 15 D14
Bickington 4 F1
Bicton 20 E5
Biddenden 11 F9
Biddulph 27 K9
Bideford 6 J3
Bidford-on-Avon . . .15 A10
Bigbury on Sea 3 G14
Biggar 40 K3
Biggin Hill 10 D5
Biggleswade 16 A7
Bildeston 25 L4
Billericay 17 F11
Billesdon 22 E6
Billingborough 23 B10
Billingham 32 B6
Billinghay 29 J10
Billingshurst 10 G1
Bilston 21 G10
Binbrook 29 E11
Bingham 22 B5
Bingley 27 B12
Birchgrove 13 G10
Birchington 11 C14
Birdlip 15 E8
Birkdale 26 D4
Birkenhead 26 G4
Birmingham 21 H11
Birtley
Northumb 36 F7
T&W 37 H11
Bishop Auckland 32 B4
Bishopbriggs 39 C11
Bishop Monkton 32 H5
Bishop's Castle 20 H4
Bishop's Cleeve 15 D8
Bishop's Frome 14 B5
Bishops Lydeard . . . 7 J10
Bishop's Nympton . . . 6 J6
Bishop's Stortford . .17 C9
Bishop's Tawton 6 J4
Bishopsteignton . . . 4 F3
Bishopstoke 9 F9
Bishopston 13 H9
Bishop's Waltham . . . 9 F10
Bitton 14 K5
Blaby 22 F4
Blackburn 26 C7
Blackfield 9 G9
Blackford
Cumb 36 G2
Perth 45 J11

Blackpool 26 B4
Blackridge 39 D13
Blackwall Tunnel . . .10 B4
Blackwaterfoot 38 H4
Blackwood
Caerph 7 B10
S Lanark 39 F12
Blaenau Ffestiniog . .18 F7
Blaenavon 14 F1
Blaengraw 13 G13
Blagdon 7 F14
Blaina 7 A11
Blair Atholl 45 C10
Blairgowrie 45 E13
Blakeney
Glos 14 F5
Norf 24 A5
Blanchand 37 H8
Blandford Forum 8 G3
Blaydon 37 G10
Bleadon 7 F12
Blean 11 D12
Bletchingdon 15 E14
Bletchley 16 B3
Blewbury 15 H14
Blidworth 28 J5
Blindburn 36 B7
Blisworth 22 K6
Blockley 15 C10
Blofield 24 D8
Bloxham 15 C13
Blubberhouses 32 J3
Blundeston 24 F10
Blyth
Northumb 37 E12
Notts 28 F5
Blyth Bridge 40 J4
Blythburgh 25 H9
Blyton 28 F7
Boath 48 A6
Boat of Garten 49 G10
Boddam
Aberds 50 C10
Shetland 57 L5
Bodedern 18 C3
Bodenham 14 A4
Bodiam 11 G8
Bodinnick 3 F9
Bodmin 3 E8
Bognor Regis 9 H14
Boldon 37 G12
Bollington 27 H10
Bolney 10 G3
Bolsover 28 G3
Bolton 27 E8
Bolton Abbey 32 J2
Bolton Bridge 32 J2
Bolton by Bowland . .31 K13
Bolton le Sands 31 H10
Bonarbridge 52 J8
Bonawe 44 F2
Bonby 29 C8
Bonchester Bridge . .36 B4
Bonchurch 9 K10
Bordon 9 D13
Borehamwood 16 F6
Boreland 35 D12
Borgh 55 B6
Borgue 34 J7
Boroughbridge 32 H5
Borough Green 10 D7
Borrowdale 31 C8
Borth 19 M6
Bosbury 14 B6
Boscastle 3 C8
Bosham 9 G13
Boston 23 A12
Boston Spa 32 K6
Botesdale 24 H5

Bothel 35 J12
Bothenhampton 5 E8
Botley 15 F13
Bottesford 22 B7
Bottisham 23 J14
Botwnnog 18 G2
Bourne 23 C9
Bourne End 16 G4
Bournemouth 8 H5
Bourton-on-the-
Water 15 D10
Bovey Tracey 4 F2
Bow 4 D1
Bowes 32 C2
Bowmore 43 N5
Bowness-on-
Solway 35 G13
Bowness-on-
Windermere 31 E10
Box 14 K7
Bozeat 23 K8
Brabourne 11 E11
Brabourne Lees 11 F11
Bracadale 47 H3
Bracebridge Heath . .29 H8
Bracklesham 9 H13
Brackley
Northants 15 C15
Northants 16 B1
Bracknell 16 J3
Braco 45 J10
Bradford 27 B12
Bradford-on-Avon . . . 8 A3
Brading 9 J11
Bradpole 5 D8
Bradwell Waterside . .25 Q5
Bradworthy 6 K2
Brae 57 F4
Braeantra 48 A6
Braemar 49 J12
Braemore
Highland 48 A3
Highland 53 F12
Brae Roy Lodge 48 J4
Brailsford 21 B13
Braintree 17 C12
Bramford 25 L6
Bramhall 27 G9
Bramhope 27 A13
Brampton
Cambs 23 H11
Cumb 36 G4
Brancaster 24 A2
Branderburgh 49 A13
Brandon
Durham 37 J11
Suff 24 G2
Branston 29 H9
Brantham 25 M6
Bratton Fleming 6 H5
Braunston 22 J4
Braunton 6 H3
Bray 16 H4
Breage 2 J4
Breakish 47 J6
Bream 14 F5
Breanais 55 E2
Brechfa 13 C9
Brechin 51 L5
Breck of Cruan 56 E3
Brecon 13 D14
Brede 11 H9
Bredenbury 14 A5
Bremirehoull 57 K5
Brent 10 A3
Brentwood 17 F11
Bretforton 15 B9
Brewood 21 F9
Bride 30 E4
Bridestowe 3 C13
Bridge 11 D12
Bridgend
Argyll 43 M5
Bridgend 13 J13
Bridge of Allan 39 A12
Bridge of Balgie 44 E7
Bridge of Cally 45 D13
Bridge of Don 50 F8
Bridge of Earn 45 H13

Bridge of Orchy 44 E5
Bridge of Weir 39 D8
Bridgnorth 21 G8
Bridgwater 7 H12
Bridlington 33 H13
Bridport 5 D8
Brierfield 27 B9
Brierley Hill 21 H10
Brigg 29 D9
Brighouse 27 C12
Brighstone 9 J9
Brightlingsea 25 P5
Brighton 10 J4
Brigstock 23 G8
Brill 16 D1
Brimfield 20 K6
Brinian 56 D4
Brinklow 22 H3
Brinkworth 15 H9
Bristol 14 J4
Briston 24 B5
Briton Ferry 13 G11
Brixham 4 H3
Brixton 3 F13
Brixworth 22 H6
Brize Norton 15 F11
Broad Chalke 8 E5
Broadclyst 4 D3
Broadford 47 J6
Broad Haven 12 E2
Broadhembury 4 C4
Broad Hinton 15 J10
Broadmayne 5 E11
Broadstairs 11 C15
Broadstone 8 H4
Broadwas 14 A6
Broadway 15 C10
Broadwey 5 E10
Broadwindsor 5 C8
Brochel 46 G5
Brockenhurst 9 G8
Brockworth 15 E8
Brocton 21 E10
Brodick 38 G5
Bromfield 20 J5
Bromham
Bedford 23 K8
Wilts 8 A4
Bromley 10 C5
Bromley Green 11 F10
Brompton 32 E5
Brompton Regis 4 A3
Bromsgrove 21 J10
Bromyard 14 A5
Brooke 24 F7
Broomfield 17 D12
Broomhaugh 37 G9
Broomhill 37 C11
Brora 53 H10
Broseley 20 F7
Brothertoft 29 K11
Brotton 33 B8
Brough
Cumb 31 C14
E Yorks 29 B8
Highland 53 A14
Shetland 57 E5
Broughton
Borders 40 K4
Hants 9 D8
Lancs 26 B6
N Lincs 29 D8
Northants 22 H7
Broughton Astley . . .22 F4
Broughton-in-
Furness 31 F8
Broughty Ferry 51 P3
Brownhills 21 F11
Broxburn 40 F3
Broxton 20 A5
Bruichladdich 43 M4
Brundall 24 E8
Brunton
Northumb 37 A11
Northumb 37 F8
Bruton 8 D2
Brymbo 20 A3
Brynamman 13 E11
Bryncrug 19 K6

Brynmawr 13 E15
Brynsiencyn 18 D4
Bubwith 28 A6
Buchlyvie 39 A10
Buckden
Cambs 23 J10
N Yorks 32 G1
Buckfast 4 G1
Buckfastleigh 4 G1
Buckhaven 40 D6
Buckie 50 A3
Buckingham 16 B2
Buckland 15 G12
Buckland Brewer 6 K3
Buckland Newton . . . 5 C10
Buckley 26 J3
Bucksburn 50 F8
Buck's Cross 6 J2
Bude 3 A10
Budleigh Salterton . . 4 F4
Bugbrooke 22 K5
Bugle 3 F8
Builth Wells 13 A14
Bulford 8 C6
Bulkington 22 G2
Bulwell 22 A4
Bunbury 26 K6
Bunessan 42 F5
Bungay 24 G8
Bunnahabhain 43 L6
Buntingford 17 C8
Bunwell 24 F6
Burbage
Derbys 27 H11
Leics 22 F3
Wilts 8 B7
Bures 25 M4
Burford 15 E11
Burgess Hill 10 H4
Burgh-by-Sands 36 H2
Burghclere 9 A9
Burghead 49 B12
Burghfield Common . .16 J1
Burgh le Marsh 29 H14
Burley
Hants 8 G7
W Yorks 32 K3
Burlton 20 D5
Burneside 31 E11
Burness 56 B6
Burnham 16 G4
Burnham Market 24 A3
Burnham-on-
Crouch 17 F14
Burnham-on-Sea . . . 7 G12
Burniston 33 E12
Burnley 27 B9
Burnmouth 41 G12
Burntisland 40 E5
Burntwood 21 F11
Burrafirth 57 A7
Burravoe 57 D6
Burrelton 45 F14
Burry Port
Carms 12 G8
Carms 13 G8
Burscough Bridge . . .26 D5
Burstwick 29 B11
Burton 31 G11
Burton Agnes 33 H13
Burton Bradstock . . . 5 E8
Burton Fleming 33 G12
Burton in Lonsdale . .31 G12
Burton Latimer 22 H7
Burton upon Stather . 28 C7
Burton upon Trent . . .21 D13
Burwash 10 G7
Burwell 23 J14
Burwick 56 H4
Bury 27 E9
Bury St Edmunds . . .25 J3
Bushey 16 F6
Buttermere 30 C7
Buxted 10 G6
Buxton 27 H11
Byfield 15 A14
Byfleet 16 J5
Bylchau 18 D9

Cabrach 50 E2
Caenby Corner 29 F8
Caergwrle 20 A4
Caerleon 7 C12
Caernarfon 18 D4
Caerphilly 7 C10
Caersws 19 L10
Caerwent 14 G3
Cairinis 54 C5
Cairndow 44 H3
Cairngaan 34 K2
Cairnryan 34 G1
Caister-on-Sea . . 24 D10
Caistor 29 D10
Calanais 55 D4
Caldbeck 36 J2
Calder Bridge 30 D6
Caldercruix 39 D13
Caldicot 14 H3
Calfsound 56 C5
Calgary 42 C5
Callander 45 J8
Callington 3 E11
Calne 15 J9
Calshot 9 H9
Calstock 3 E12
Calverton 28 K5
Cam 14 G6
Camber 11 H10
Camberley 16 K3
Cambo 37 E9
Camborne 2 H4
Cambourne 23 K12
Cambridge 23 K13
Camden 10 A3
Camelford 3 C9
Cammachmore 51 H8
Campbeltown 38 H2
Camrose 12 E3
Canisbay 53 A15
Cannich 48 E4
Cannington 7 H11
Cannock 21 F10
Canonbie 36 F2
Canterbury 11 D12
Cantley 24 E8
Canvey Island 17 G13
Caol 44 B3
Caolas Stocinis 55 H3
Caoles 42 D2
Capel 10 F2
Capel Curig 18 E7
Capel St Mary 25 M6
Carbis Bay 2 H3
Carbost
  Highland 46 G4
  Highland 47 H3
Cardiff 7 D10
Cardigan 12 B5
Cardington 16 A5
Cardross 39 C8
Cargill 45 F13
Carhampton 7 G9
Carisbrooke 9 J9
Cark 31 G9
Carlabhagh 55 C4
Carleton Rode 24 F6
Carlisle 36 H3
Carlops 40 H4
Carlton
  Notts 22 A5
  N Yorks 28 B5
Carlton Colville 24 G10
Carlton-in-Lindrick . 28 F4
Carlton Miniott 32 F6
Carluke 39 E13
Carmarthen 12 E8
Carmyllie 51 N4
Carnachuin 49 J9
Carnforth 31 G11
Carno 19 L9
Carnoustie 51 P4
Carnwath 40 J2
Carradale 38 G3
Carrbridge 49 F10
Carrick 38 A7

Carronbridge 35 D9
Carsaig 42 F7
Carskiey 38 K1
Carsphairn 34 D6
Carstairs 40 J2
Carterton 15 F11
Cartmel 31 G9
Castle Acre 24 D3
Castlebay / Bagh a
  Chaisteil 54 K3
Castle Cary 8 D1
Castle Donington . . . 22 C3
Castle Douglas 35 G8
Castleford 28 B3
Castlemartin 12 G3
Castleside 37 J9
Castleton
  Derbys 27 G12
  N Yorks 33 D8
Castletown
  Highland 53 B14
  IoM 30 J2
Caston 24 F4
Castor 23 F10
Catcleugh 36 C6
Caterham 10 D4
Caton 31 H11
Catrine 39 H10
Catsfield 11 H8
Catterall 26 A6
Catterick 32 E4
Catterick Camp 32 E3
Catton 36 H7
Caulkerbush 35 H10
Cawdor 49 C9
Cawood 28 A4
Cawston 24 C6
Caythorpe 29 K8
Ceann Tarabhaigh . . 55 F14
Cefn-mawr 20 B3
Cemaes 18 A3
Cemmaes Road 19 K8
Cenarth 12 B6
Ceres 40 B7
Cerne Abbas 5 C10
Cerrigydrudion 18 F9
Chacewater 2 G5
Chaddesley Corbet . . 21 J9
Chadwell St Mary . . 17 H11
Chagford 3 C14
Chalfont St Giles . . . 16 F4
Chalford 15 F8
Chalgrove 16 F1
Challacombe 6 H5
Chalton 11 E11
Chandler's Ford 9 E9
Channel Tunnel 11 F12
Chapel en le Frith . . 27 G11
Chapel St Leonards 29 G14
Chapeltown
  S Lanark 39 F11
  S Yorks 28 E2
Chard 4 C7
Charing 11 E10
Charlbury 15 E12
Charlestown of
  Aberlour 49 D13
Charlton 15 H8
Charlton Horethorne 5 A10
Charlton Kings 15 E8
Charlwood 10 E3
Charminster 5 D10
Charmouth 4 D7
Chartham 11 D12
Chatham 17 J12
Chathill 37 A10
Chatteris 23 G12
Chatton 37 A9
Chawleigh 4 C1
Cheadle
  Gtr Manchester 27 G9
  Staffs 21 B11
Chedburgh 25 K2
Cheddar 7 F13
Cheddleton 21 A10
Chellaston 22 B2
Chelmarsh 21 H8
Chelmsford 17 E12
Cheltenham 15 D8

Chepstow 14 G4
Cherhill 15 K9
Cheriton 9 E11
Cheriton Fitzpaine . . 4 C2
Chertsey 16 J5
Chesham 16 E4
Cheshunt 17 E8
Chester 26 J5
Chesterfield 28 G2
Chester-le-Street . . 37 H11
Chew Magna 7 E14
Chewton Mendip . . . 7 F14
Chichester 9 G13
Chiddingfold 9 D14
Chideock 5 D8
Chigwell 17 F9
Chilcompton 8 B1
Chilham 11 D11
Chillington 4 J1
Chilton 32 A4
Chingford 17 F8
Chinnor 16 E2
Chippenham 15 J8
Chipping Campden . 15 C10
Chipping Norton . . . 15 D12
Chipping Ongar . . . 17 E10
Chipping Sodbury . . 14 H6
Chirbury 20 G3
Chirk 20 C3
Chirnside 41 H11
Chiseldon 15 J10
Chitterne 8 C4
Chobham 16 J4
Chollerton 37 F8
Cholsey 15 H4
Chorley 26 D6
Chorleywood 16 F5
Christchurch
  Cambs 23 F13
  Dorset 8 H6
Christow 4 E2
Chudleigh 4 F2
Chulmleigh 6 K5
Churchdown 14 E7
Churchill 15 D11
Churchstow 4 J1
Church Stretton 20 G5
Church Village 7 C9
Chwilog 18 G4
Cilgerran 12 B5
Cille Bhrighde 54 H4
Cilycwm 13 C11
Cinderford 14 E5
Cirencester 15 F9
City of London 10 A4
Clachan
  Argyll 38 E2
  Highland 47 H5
Clachan na Luib 54 C5
Clackmannan 40 D2
Clacton-on-Sea 25 P6
Cladich 44 G2
Claggan 42 D9
Claigan 46 F2
Clanfield 9 F12
Claonaig 38 E3
Clapham
  Bedford 23 K9
  N Yorks 31 H13
Clare 25 L2
Clashmore 53 K9
Clavering 17 C9
Claverley 21 G8
Clawton 3 B11
Clay Cross 28 H2
Claydon 25 K6
Claypole 28 K7
Cleadale 47 N4
Cleat 56 H4
Cleator Moor 30 C6
Cleethorpes 29 D11
Cleeve Prior 15 A10
Clehonger 14 C3
Cleobury Mortimer . 20 J7
Clevedon 7 D13
Cleveleys 26 A4
Cley 24 A5
Cliffe 17 H12
Clifford 14 B1

Clipston 22 G6
Clipstone 28 H4
Clitheroe 27 A8
Clive 20 D6
Clophill 16 B5
Closeburn 35 D9
Cloughton 33 E12
Clova 51 K2
Clovelly 6 J2
Clovenfords 40 K7
Clowne 28 G3
Clun 20 H4
Clunbury 20 H4
Clunes 48 K3
Clungunford 20 J4
Clutton 8 B1
Clydach 13 F10
Clydebank 39 D10
Clynnog-fawr 18 F4
Clyro 14 B1
Coalbrookdale 20 F7
Coalburn 39 G13
Coalville 22 D3
Coatbridge 39 D12
Cobham
  Kent 17 J11
  Sur 10 D2
Cock Bridge 49 G13
Cockburnspath 41 F10
Cockenzie 40 F7
Cockerham 31 J10
Cockermouth 30 A7
Cockfield
  Durham 32 B3
  Suff 25 K4
Cockshutt 20 D5
Coddenham 25 K6
Codford St Mary 8 D4
Coggeshall 25 N3
Coignafearn Lodge . 48 G7
Coille Mhorgil 48 H1
Coillore 47 H3
Colby 30 J2
Colchester 25 N5
Cold Ashton 14 J6
Coldingham 41 G12
Coldstream 41 J11
Coleford
  Devon 4 D1
  Glos 14 F4
Coleshill 21 H13
Colinton 40 G5
Colintraive 38 C5
Colliston 50 E9
Collin 35 F11
Collingbourne
  Kingston 8 B7
Collingham
  Notts 28 H7
  W Yorks 32 K5
Colmonel 34 E2
Colne 27 B10
Colpy 50 D5
Colsterworth 23 C8
Coltishall 24 C7
Colwell 37 F8
Colwich 21 D11
Colwyn Bay 18 C8
Colyton 4 D6
Combe Martin 6 G4
Comberton 23 K12
Combwich 7 G11
Compton
  W Berks 15 J14
  W Sus 9 F12
Compton Martin 7 F14
Comrie 45 G9
Condover 20 F5
Congleton 27 J9
Congresbury 7 E13
Coningsby 29 J11
Conisbrough 28 E4
Coniston 31 E8
Connah's Quay 26 J3
Connel 44 F1
Connel Park 34 B7
Cononbridge 48 C6
Consett 37 H10
Contin 48 C5

Conwy 18 C7
Cookham 16 G4
Coolham 10 G2
Coombe Bissett 8 E6
Copplestone 4 C1
Coppull 26 D6
Copthorne 10 F4
Corbridge 37 G8
Corby 22 G7
Corby Glen 23 C9
Corfe Castle 8 J4
Corfe Mullen 8 H4
Cornhill on Tweed . . 41 K11
Corpach 44 B2
Corran 44 C2
Corrie 38 F5
Corringham
  Lincs 28 E7
  Thurrock 17 G12
Corris 19 K7
Corsham 14 J7
Corsley 8 C3
Corsock 35 F8
Corton 24 F10
Corwen 18 F10
Coryton 17 G12
Coseley 21 G10
Cosham 9 G11
Costessey 24 D6
Cotgrave 22 B5
Cotherstone 32 B2
Cottenham 23 J13
Cottered 17 C8
Cottesmore 23 D8
Cottingham 29 A9
Coulags 46 G9
Coulport 38 B7
Countesthorpe 22 F4
Coupar Angus 45 E14
Cove
  Argyll 38 B7
  Highland 46 B8
Cove Bay 50 G8
Coventry 22 H2
Coverack 2 K5
Cowbit 23 D11
Cowbridge 13 J13
Cowdenbeath 40 D4
Cowes 9 H9
Cowfold 10 G3
Cowpen 37 E11
Cowplain 9 F11
Coxheath 11 D8
Coylton 34 A5
Craggie 49 E8
Crai 13 D12
Craibstone 50 B3
Craigellachie 49 D13
Craighouse 43 M7
Craigmore 38 D6
Craignure 42 E9
Craigtown 53 C11
Crail 41 C9
Cramlington 37 F11
Cranborne 8 F5
Cranbrook 11 F8
Cranleigh 10 F1
Cranmore 8 C1
Cranstal 30 E4
Cranwell 29 K9
Crathie 49 J13
Craven Arms 20 H5
Crawford 35 A10
Crawfordjohn 39 H13
Crawley 10 F3
Creag Ghoraidh 54 E5
Creake 24 B3
Credenhill 14 B3
Crediton 4 D2
Creetown 34 H5
Cressage 20 F7
Cresselly 12 F4
Crewe 21 A8
Crewkerne 5 C8
Crianlarich 44 G5
Criccieth 18 G5

Crick 22 H4
Crickhowell 14 E1
Cricklade 15 G10
Crieff 45 G10
Crimond 50 B9
Crinan 38 A2
Crocketford 35 F9
Croggan 42 F9
Croglin 36 J4
Croick 52 J6
Cromarty 49 B8
Cromer 24 A7
Cromor 55 E6
Crondall 9 C12
Crook 37 K10
Crookham 41 K12
Crooklands 31 F11
Crosbost 55 E6
Crosby 35 J11
Crosby Ravensworth 31 C12
Cross-Hands 13 E9
Crosshill 34 C4
Crossmichael 35 G8
Croston 26 D5
Crowborough 10 F6
Crowland 23 D11
Crowle 28 C6
Crowthorne 16 J3
Croxton Kerrial 22 C7
Croyde 6 H3
Croydon 10 C4
Cruden Bay 50 D9
Crudgington 20 E7
Crulabhig 55 D3
Crymych 12 C5
Cuaig 46 F7
Cuan 42 G9
Cuckfield 10 G4
Cuddington
- Bucks 16 D2
- Ches W 26 H6
Cudworth 28 C2
Cuffley 17 E8
Culgaith 31 A12
Culkein 52 E2
Cullen 50 A4
Cullicudden 48 B7
Cullivoe 57 B6
Culloden 49 D8
Cullompton 4 C4
Culmazie 34 H4
Culmington 20 H5
Culmstock 4 B5
Culrain 52 J7
Cults 50 G7
Cumbernauld 39 C12
Cuminestown 50 B7
Cummertrees 35 G12
Cumnock 34 A6
Cumnor 15 F13
Cumwhinton 36 H3
Cupar 40 B6
Currie 40 G4
Curry Rivel 7 J12
Cwmafan 13 G11
Cwmann 13 B9
Cwmbran 7 B11
Cwrt 19 K7
Cymmer 13 G12
Cynwyl Elfed 12 D7

D

Dagenham 17 G10
Dail bho Dheas 55 A6
Dailly 34 C3
Dalabrog 54 G4
Dalbeattie 35 G9
Dale 12 F2
Dale of Walls 57 G2
Dalguise 45 E11
Dalhalvaig 53 C11
Dalkeith 40 G6
Dallas 49 C12
Dalleagles 34 B6
Dalmally 44 G3
Dalmellington 34 C5
Dalnaspidal 45 B8
Dalnessie 52 G8
Dalry 38 F7
Dalrymple 34 B4
Dalston 36 H2
Dalton
- Dumfries 35 F12
- Northumb 37 H8
- N Yorks 32 D5
Dalton-in-Furness 31 G8
Dalwhinnie 45 A8
Damerham 8 F6
Danbury 17 E13
Darlington 32 C4
Dartford 17 H10
Dartford Crossing 17 H10
Dartington 4 G1
Dartmouth 4 H2
Darton 28 C2
Darvel 39 G10
Darwen 26 C7
Daventry 22 J4
Davington 35 C13
Dawlish 4 F3
Deal 11 D14
Dearham 35 K11
Dearne 28 D3
Debenham 25 J6
Deddington 15 C13
Deeping St Nicholas 23 D11
Deerness 56 F5
Deganwy 18 C7
Delabole 3 C8
Delchirach 49 E12
Delves 37 H10
Denbigh 18 D10
Denby Dale 27 E13
Denholm 36 B4
Denny 39 B13
Dent 31 F13
Denton
- Grt Manchester 27 F10
- Lincs 22 B7
Derby 22 B2
Dereham 24 D4
Dersingham 24 B1
Dervaig 42 C6
Desborough 22 G6
Desford 22 E3
Devil's Bridge 19 N7
Devizes 8 A5
Devonport 3 F12
Dewsbury 27 C13
Diabaig 46 E8
Dibden Purlieu 9 G9
Dickleborough 24 G6
Didcot 15 H14
Digby 29 J9
Dinas Mawddwy 19 J8
Dinas Powis 7 D10
Dingwall 48 C6
Dinnington 28 F4
Dinton 8 D5
Dippen 38 H5
Dirleton 41 E8
Diss 24 G6
Distington 30 B6
Ditchingham 24 F8
Ditchling 10 H4
Dittisham 4 H2
Ditton Priors 20 H7
Dobwalls 3 E10
Docking 24 B2
Dockray 31 B9
Doddinghurst 17 F10
Doddington
- Cambs 23 F12
- Northumb 41 K12
Dolanog 20 E1
Dolfor 20 H2
Dolgarrog 18 D7
Dolgellau 19 J7
Dollar 40 D2
Dolphinton 40 J4
Dolton 6 K4
Dolwyddelan 18 E7
Doncaster 28 D4
Donhead StAndrew 8 E4
Donington 23 B11
Donnington 21 E8
Dorchester
- Dorset 5 E10
- Oxon 15 G14
Dores 48 E7
Dorking 10 E2
Dornie 47 J8
Dornoch 53 K9
Dorridge 21 J12
Dorstone 14 B2
Douglas
- IoM 30 H3
- S Lanark 39 G13
Dounby 56 D2
Doune 45 J9
Dounreay 53 B11
Dove Holes 27 H11
Dover 11 E14
Doveridge 21 C12
Downham 23 G14
Downham Market 24 E1
Downton 8 E6
Drayton 24 D6
Dreghorn 39 G8
Drem 41 F8
Driffield 33 J12
Drigg 30 D6
Drimnin 42 C7
Droitwich Spa 21 K10
Dronfield 28 G2
Drongan 34 B5
Druid 18 F10
Drumbeg 52 E3
Drumgask 48 J7
Drumjohn 34 D6
Drummore 34 K2
Drumnadrochit 48 E6
Drymen 39 B9
Drynoch 47 H4
Duchally 52 G5
Duddington 23 E8
Dudley 21 G10
Duffield 22 A2
Dufftown 50 D2
Dukinfield 27 F10
Dullingham 25 K1
Dulnain Bridge 49 F10
Duloe 3 F10
Dulverton 4 A3
Dumbarton 39 C9
Dumfries 35 F10
Dunans 38 A5
Dunbar 41 F9
Dunbeath 53 F13
Dunblane 45 J9
Dunchurch 22 H3
Dundee 51 P2
Dundonald 39 G8
Dundrennan 35 J8
Dunecht 50 G6
Dunfermline 40 E4
Dungraggan 44 J7
Dunino 41 B8
Dunipace 39 B13
Dunkeld 45 E12
Dunlop 39 F9
Dunnet 53 B14
Dunning 45 H12
Dunnington 33 J8
Dunoon 38 C6
Dunragit 34 H2
Duns 41 H10
Dunsby 23 C10
Dunscore 35 E9
Dunsford 4 E2
Dunstable 16 C5
Dunster 7 G8
Dunston 21 E10
Dunsyre 40 J3
Dunure 34 B3
Dunvegan 46 G2
Dunwich 25 J9
Durham 37 J11
Durness 52 B6
Durrington 8 C6
Dursley 14 G6
Dyce 50 F7
Dykehead 51 L2
Dymchurch 11 G12
Dymock 14 C5
Dysart 40 D6
Dyserth 26 H1

E

Eaglescliffe 32 C6
Eaglesfield 35 F13
Eaglesham 39 E10
Eakring 28 H5
Ealing 10 B2
Earby 27 A10
Eardisley 14 B2
Earith 23 H12
Earls Barton 22 J7
Earl's Colne 25 N3
Earlsferry 41 C8
Earl Shilton 22 F3
Earl Soham 25 J7
Earlston 41 K8
Earsdon 37 F12
Easdale 42 G9
Easebourne 9 E14
Easington
- Durham 37 J13
- E Yorks 29 C12
Easington Colliery 37 J13
Easingwold 32 G7
East Bergholt 25 M5
East Boldre 9 H8
Eastbourne 10 K7
East Brent 7 F12
East Bridgford 22 A5
East Calder 40 G3
Eastchurch 11 B11
East Cowes 9 H10
East Cowton 32 D4
East Dean 10 K6
Easter Skeld 57 H4
Eastfield 33 F12
East Grinstead 10 F4
East Harling 24 G4
East Horsley 10 D1
East Ilsley 15 H14
East Kilbride 39 E11
East Leake 22 C4
Eastleigh 9 F9
East Linton 41 F8
East Looe 3 F10
East Markham 28 G6
Eastnor 14 C6
East Norton 22 E6
East Oakley 9 C10
Easton
- Dorset 5 F10
- Northants 23 E9
Easton-in-Gordano 14 J4
Eastry 11 D14
East Wemyss 40 D6
East Wittering 9 H13
East Witton 32 F3
Eastwood 28 K3
East Woodhay 9 A9
Eaton 22 C6
Eaton Socon 23 K10
Ebberston 33 F11
Ebbw Vale 7 A10
Ecclaw 41 G10
Ecclefechan 35 F12
Eccleshall 21 D9
Eccleston 26 A5
Echt 50 G6
Eckington
- Derbys 28 G3
- Worcs 15 B8
Edderton 53 K9
Edenbridge 10 E5
Edgmond 21 E8
Edinburgh 40 F5
Edington 8 B4
Edmundbyers 37 J9
Edwinstowe 28 H5
Edzell 51 L5
Egham 16 J5
Eglwyswrw 12 C5
Egremont 30 C6
Egton 33 D10
Eilean Iarmain 47 K7
Eisgean 55 F5
Elan Village 19 P9
Elgin 49 B13
Elgol 47 K5
Elham 11 E12
Elie 40 C7
Elishaw 36 D7
Elland 27 C12
Ellesmere 20 C5
Ellesmere Port 26 H4
Ellington 37 D11
Ellon 50 D8
Elmswell 25 J4
Elphin 52 G4
Elsdon 37 D8
Elsenham 17 C10
Elstead 9 C14
Elston 22 A6
Elvanfoot 35 B10
Elveden 24 H3
Elvington 33 K8
Elworth 27 J8
Ely 23 G14
Embleton 37 A11
Embo 53 J10
Empingham 23 E8
Emsworth 9 G12
Enderby 22 F4
Endon 21 A10
Enfield 17 F8
Enstone 15 D12
Enterkinfoot 35 C9
Epping 17 E9
Epsom 10 D3
Epworth 28 D6
Eriboll 52 C6
Errogie 48 F6
Errol 45 G14
Erskine 39 C9
Erskine Bridge 39 C9
Escrick 33 K8
Esher 10 C2
Esh Winning 37 J10
Eskdalemuir 35 D13
Eston 32 B7
Etchingham 11 G8
Eton 16 H4
Ettington 15 B11
Etwall 21 C13
Euxton 26 C6
Evanton 48 B7
Evercreech 8 D1
Everleigh 8 B7
Evershot 5 C9
Evesham 15 B9
Ewell 10 C3
Ewhurst 10 F1
Ewyas Harold 14 D2
Exbourne 3 A14
Exeter 4 D3
Exford 6 H7
Exminster 4 E3
Exmouth 4 F3
Exton 23 D8
Eyam 27 H13
Eye
- Pboro 23 E11
- Suff 25 H6
Eyemouth 41 G12
Eyethorne 11 E13
Eynsford 10 C6
Eynsham 15 F13

F

Faddiley 20 A6
Fairbourne 19 J6
Fairford 15 F10
Fairlie 38 E7
Fairlight 11 H9
Fakenham 24 B4
Fala 40 G7
Faldingworth 29 F9
Falkirk 39 B13

Falkland 40 C5
Falmer 10 J4
Falmouth 2 H6
Falstone 36 E6
Fareham 9 G10
Faringdon 15 G11
Farnborough
  Hants 9 B13
  W Berks 15 H13
Farndon 20 A5
Farnham 9 C13
Farnworth 27 E8
Farr 48 E7
Fasag 46 F9
Faslane 38 A7
Fauldhouse 40 G2
Faversham 11 C11
Fawley 9 G9
Fazeley 21 F13
Fearn 49 A9
Fearnan 45 E9
Feckenham 21 K11
Felixstowe 25 M8
Felton 37 C10
Feltwell 24 F2
Fenny Bentley 21 A12
Fenny Compton 15 A13
Fenny Stratford 16 B3
Fenwick 39 F9
Feock 2 H6
Feolin Ferry 43 M6
Ferndown 8 H5
Ferness 49 D10
Fernhurst 9 E14
Ferryhill 32 A4
Ferryside 12 F7
Fettercairn 51 K5
Filby 24 D9
Filey 33 F13
Fillongley 21 H13
Filton 14 J5
Fincham 24 E1
Finchingfield 17 B11
Finchley 16 F7
Findhorn 49 B11
Findochty 50 A3
Findon 10 J2
Finedon 23 H8
Finningley 28 E5
Finstown 56 E3
Fintry 39 B11
Fionnphort 42 F4
Fishbourne 9 H10
Fishguard 12 C3
Fishnish 42 D8
Fishtoft 23 A12
Flamborough 33 G14
Fleet 9 B13
Fleetwood 31 K9
Flimby 35 K11
Flint 26 H3
Flitwick 16 B5
Flodden 41 K12
Flookburgh 31 G9
Fochabers 50 B2
Foel 19 J10
Folkestone 11 F13
Folkingham 23 B9
Fontmell Magna 8 F3
Ford 43 H10
Forden 20 F3
Fordham 25 H1
Fordingbridge 8 F6
Fordyce 50 A4
Forest Row 10 F5
Forfar 51 M3
Formby 26 E3
Forres 49 C11
Forsinain 53 D11
Forsinard 53 D10
Fort Augustus 48 H4
Fort George
  Highland 49 C8
  Jersey . . . . 4 Jersey
Forth 40 H2
Forth Road Bridge . . 40 E4
Fortrie 50 C5
Fortrose 49 C8
Fortuneswell 5 F10

Fort William 44 B3
Fothergill 35 K11
Fotheringhay 23 F9
Foulden 41 H12
Foulsham 24 C5
Fountainhall 40 J7
Four Lanes 2 H4
Fovant 8 E5
Fowey 3 F9
Fownhope 14 C4
Foxdale 30 H2
Foyers 48 F6
Fraddon 2 F6
Framlingham 25 J7
Frampton on Severn . 14 F6
Frant 10 F6
Fraserburgh 50 A8
Freckleton 26 C5
Freethorpe 24 E9
Fremington 6 H4
Frensham 9 C13
Freshwater 9 J8
Freshwater East 12 G4
Fressingfield 24 H7
Freswick 53 B15
Freuchie 40 C5
Friday Bridge 23 E13
Fridaythorpe 33 H10
Frimley 9 B13
Frinton-on-Sea 25 P7
Friockheim 51 M4
Frizington 30 C6
Frodsham 26 H6
Frome 8 C2
Frongoch 18 G9
Froxfield 15 K11
Fulbourn 23 K14
Fulford 33 K8
Fulwood 26 B6
Funzie 57 C7
Furnace 44 J2
Fyfield 17 E10
Fyvie 50 D6

G

Gaerwen 18 C4
Gaick Lodge 49 K8
Gailey 21 E10
Gainford 32 C3
Gainsborough 28 F7
Gairloch 46 D8
Gairlochy 44 A3
Galashiels 40 K7
Galgate 31 J10
Galmisdale 47 N4
Galmpton 4 H2
Galston 39 G10
Gamlingay 23 K11
Garbhallt 38 A5
Garboldisham 24 G5
Gardenstown 50 A7
Garelochhead 38 A7
Garforth 28 A3
Gargrave 32 J1
Gargunnock 39 A12
Garlieston 34 J5
Garmouth 50 A2
Garrow 45 E10
Garsdale Head 31 E13
Garstang 31 K10
Garston 26 G4
Garton-on-the-
  Wolds 33 H11
Garvald 41 F8
Garvard 43 J5
Garve 48 B4
Gatehouse of Fleet . 34 H6
Gateshead 37 G11
Gatley 27 G9
Gatwick Airport 10 E3
Gawthwaite 31 F8
Gaydon 15 A12
Gayton 24 D2
Gaywood 24 C1
Gearraidh na h-
  Aibhne 55 D4
Geary 46 E2

Geddington 22 G7
Gedney 23 C13
Gedney Drove End . . 23 C13
Georgeham 6 H3
Gerrards Cross 16 G5
Gifford 41 G8
Giggleswick 31 H14
Gillingham
  Dorset 5 A11
  Medway 17 J12
Gilmerton 45 G10
Gilsland 36 G5
Gilwern 14 E1
Giosla 55 E3
Girton 23 J13
Girvan 34 D3
Gisburn 31 K14
Gladestry 14 A1
Glamis 51 N2
Glanaman 13 E10
Glanton 37 B9
Glasbury 13 C15
Glasgow 39 D10
Glasserton 34 K5
Glasson 31 J10
Glastonbury 7 H14
Glemsford 25 L3
Glenbarr 38 G1
Glenborrodale 42 B8
Glenbrittle 47 J4
Glencaple 35 G10
Glencarse 45 G14
Glencoe 44 D3
Glendoll Lodge 51 K1
Gleneagles 45 H11
Glenelg 47 K8
Glenfinnan 47 N9
Glenluce 34 H3
Glenmaye 30 G2
Glenmore Lodge . . 49 H10
Glenprosen Lodge . . 51 L1
Glenrothes 40 C5
Glenstriven 38 C5
Glentrool Village 34 F4
Glenwhilly 34 F3
Glinton 23 E10
Glossop 27 F11
Gloucester 14 E7
Glusburn 27 A11
Glutt Lodge 53 E11
Glyn Ceiriog 20 C3
Glyncorrwg 13 G12
Glynde 10 J5
Glyndyfrdwy 20 B2
Glyn Neath 13 F12
Gnosall 21 D9
Goathland 33 D10
Gobowen 20 C4
Godalming 9 C14
Godmanchester 23 H11
Godshill 9 J10
Godstone 10 E4
Goldhanger 25 Q4
Golspie 53 J10
Goodrich 14 E4
Goodwick 12 C3
Goole 28 B6
Goonhavern 2 F5
Gordon 41 J9
Gorebridge 40 G6
Gorey . . . . 5 Jersey
Goring 16 G1
Goring-by-Sea 10 J2
Gorleston-on-Sea . . 24 E10
Gorran Haven 3 H8
Gorseinon 13 G9
Gorslas 13 E9
Gosberton 23 B11
Gosfield 25 N2
Gosforth 30 D6
Gosport 9 H11
Goswick 41 J13
Gotham 22 C4
Goudhurst 11 F8
Gourdon 51 K7
Gourock 38 C7
Gowerton 13 G9
Grabhair 55 F5
Grain 11 B9

Grainthorpe 29 E12
Grampound 2 G7
Gramsdal 54 D5
Grangemouth 40 E2
Grange-over-
  Sands 31 G10
Grantham 23 B8
Grantown-on-Spey 49 F11
Grantshouse 41 G11
Grasby 29 D9
Grasmere 31 D9
Grassington 32 H2
Grateley 8 C7
Gravesend 17 H11
Grayrigg 31 E11
Grays 17 H11
Grayshott 9 D13
Great Ayton 32 C7
Great Baddow 17 E12
Great Barford 23 K10
Great Bentley 25 N6
Great Bridgeford 21 D9
Great Broughton 32 D7
Great Chesterford . . 17 A10
Great Clifton 30 B6
Great Dunmow 17 C11
Great Ellingham 24 F5
Great Gidding 23 G10
Greatham 32 B6
Great Harwood 27 B8
Great Horwood 16 B2
Great Malvern 14 B6
Great Massingham . . 24 C2
Great Missenden 16 E4
Great Oakley 25 N7
Great Sampford 17 B11
Great Shefford 15 J12
Great Shelford 23 K13
Great Somerford 15 H8
Great Staunton 23 H10
Great Torrington 6 K3
Great Wakering 17 G14
Great Waltham 17 D12
Great Witley 21 K8
Great Yarmouth 24 E10
Green Hammerton . . 32 J6
Greenhead 36 G5
Greenholm 39 G10
Greenlaw 41 J10
Greenloaning 45 J10
Greenock 38 C7
Greenodd 31 F9
Greenway 12 D4
Greenwich 10 B4
Gretna 36 G2
Gretna Green 36 G2
Gretton 23 F8
Greystoke 31 A10
Grimsby 29 D11
Gritley 56 F5
Grizebeck 31 F8
Groby 22 C4
Grove 15 G13
Grundisburgh 25 L7
Gualachulain 44 E3
Guard Bridge 40 B7
Guestling Green 11 H9
Guildford 10 E1
Guildtown 45 F13
Guilsfield 20 E3
Guisborough 33 C8
Guiseley 27 A12
Gullane 40 E7
Gunnerside 32 E1
Gunnislake 3 D12
Gunnista 57 H6
Gutcher 57 B6
Gwaun-Cae-
  Gurwen 13 E10
Gwbert 12 B5
Gweek 2 J4
Gwennap 2 H5
Gwyddelwern 18 F10
Gwytherin 18 D8
Gyre 56 F3

H

Hackney 10 A4
Hackthorpe 31 B11
Haddenham
  Bucks 16 E2
  Cambs 23 H13
Haddington 41 F8
Haddiscoe 24 F9
Hadleigh
  Essex 17 G13
  Suff 25 L5
Hadlow 10 E7
Hadnall 20 D6
Hagworthingham . . 29 H12
Hailsham 10 J6
Hainton 29 F10
Halberton 4 B4
Halesowen 21 H10
Halesworth 24 H8
Halford 15 B11
Halifax 27 C11
Halkirk 53 C13
Halland 10 H6
Hallow 14 A7
Hallworthy 3 C9
Halstead 25 M3
Halton 31 H11
Haltwhistle 36 G6
Halwill Junction 3 B12
Hambledon 9 F11
Hamble-le-Rice 9 G9
Hambleton
  Lancs 26 A4
  N Yorks 28 A4
Hamerton 23 H10
Hamilton 39 E12
Hammersmith &
  Fulham 10 B3
Hamnavoe
  Shetland 57 E6
  Shetland 57 J4
Hampstead Norreys 15 J14
Hampton in Arden . . 21 H13
Hamstreet 11 F11
Handcross 10 G3
Hannington 9 B10
Harbury 22 J2
Harby 22 B6
Hardingstone 22 K6
Harewood 27 A14
Haringey 10 A4
Harlech 18 G5
Harleston 24 G7
Harlow 17 E9
Haroldswick 57 A7
Harpenden 16 D6
Harrietfield 45 F11
Harrietsham 11 D9
Harrington 30 B5
Harris 47 M3
Harrogate 32 J4
Harrold 23 K8
Harrow 16 G6
Harston 23 K13
Hartest 25 K3
Hartfield 10 F5
Hartford 40 G2
Hartington 27 J12
Hartland 6 J1
Hartlebury 21 J9
Hartlepool 32 A7
Hartley
  Kent 17 J11
  Northumb 37 F12
Hartley Wintney 9 B12
Hartpury 14 D6
Hartshill 22 F2
Harvington 15 B9
Harwell 15 H13
Harwich 25 M7
Harworth 28 E5
Haselbury Plucknett . . 5 C8

Haslemere 9 D13
Haslingden 27 C8
Hassocks 10 H4
Hastigrow 53 C14
Hastings 11 J9
Haswell 37 J12
Hatch Beauchamp 4 B7
Hatfield
　Herts 16 E7
　S Yorks 28 D5
Hatfield Heath 17 D10
Hatfield Peverel 17 D13
Hatherleigh 3 A13
Hathersage 27 G13
Hatton
　Aberds 50 D9
　Derbys 21 C13
Haughley 25 J5
Haugh of Urr 35 G8
Haughton 21 D9
Havant 9 G12
Haverfordwest 12 E3
Haverhill 17 A11
Haverigg 30 F7
Havering 17 G10
Hawarden 26 J4
Hawes 31 E14
Hawick 36 B4
Hawkchurch 4 D7
Hawkesbury Upton . . 14 H6
Hawkhurst 11 G8
Hawkinge 11 F13
Hawkshead 31 E9
Hawnby 32 E7
Haworth 27 B11
Hawsker 33 D11
Haxby 33 J8
Haxey 28 D6
Haydon Bridge 36 G7
Hayfield 27 G11
Hayle 2 H3
Hay-on-Wye 14 B1
Hayton
　Cumb 36 H4
　E Yorks 33 K10
Haywards Heath 10 G4
Hazel Grove 27 G10
Hazlemere 16 F4
Heacham 24 B1
Headcorn 11 E9
Headley 9 D13
Heanor 22 A3
Heath End 9 A10
Heathfield 10 H6
Heathrow Airport . . . 16 H5
Hebburn 37 G12
Hebden Bridge 27 C10
Heckington 23 A10
Hedge End 9 F10
Hednesford 21 E11
Hedon 29 B10
Heighington 32 B4
Heilam 52 B6
Helensburgh 39 B8
Hellifield 31 J14
Helmsdale 53 G12
Helmsley 33 F8
Helperby 32 G6
Helpringham 23 A10
Helsby 26 H5
Helston 2 J4
Hemel Hempstead . . 16 E5
Hemingbrough 28 A5
Hempnall 24 F7
Hempton 24 C4
Hemsby 24 D9
Hemsworth 28 C3
Hemyock 4 B5
Henfield 10 H3
Hengoed 7 B10
Henley-in-Arden . . 21 K12
Henley-on-Thames . 16 G2
Henllan 18 D10
Henlow 16 B6
Henstridge 5 B11
Herbrandston 12 F2

Hereford 14 C4
Heriot 40 H7
Hermitage 15 J14
Herne Bay 11 C12
Herstmonceux 10 H7
Herston 56 G4
Hertford 17 D8
Hessle 29 B9
Heswall 26 G3
Hethersett 24 E6
Hetton-le-Hole 37 J12
Hexham 37 G8
Heybridge 17 E13
Heysham 31 H10
Heytesbury 8 C4
Heywood 27 D9
Hibaldstow 29 D8
Higham 17 H12
Higham Ferrers 23 J8
High Bentham 31 G12
High Bickington 6 K4
Highbridge 7 G12
Highclere 9 B9
High Ercall 20 E7
High Hesket 36 J3
High Legh 27 G8
Highley 21 H8
Hightae 35 F11
Highworth 15 G11
High Wycombe 16 F3
Hilborough 24 E3
Hildenborough 10 E6
Hilgay 24 F1
Hillingdon 16 G5
Hillington 24 C2
Hillswick 57 E3
Hilmarton 15 J9
Hilton 21 C13
Hinckley 22 F3
Hinderwell 33 C10
Hindhead 9 D13
Hindley 26 E7
Hindon 8 D4
Hingham 24 E5
Hinstock 20 D8
Hirwaun 13 F13
Histon 23 J13
Hitchin 16 B6
Hockley 17 F13
Hockliffe 16 C4
Hoddesdon 17 E8
Hodnet 20 D7
Hoff 31 C12
Holbeach 23 C12
Holbeach Drove . . . 23 D12
Holbrook 25 M6
Holford 7 G10
Holkham 24 A3
Holland-on-Sea 25 P7
Hollandstoun 56 A7
Hollym 29 B12
Holme-on-Spalding-
　moor 28 A7
Holmer 14 B4
Holmes Chapel 27 J8
Holmfirth 27 E12
Holsworthy 3 A11
Holt
　Norf 24 B5
　Wrex 20 A5
Holyhead 18 B2
Holywell 26 H2
Honington 23 A8
Honiton 4 D5
Hook 9 B12
Hook Norton 15 C12
Hope 26 K4
Hopeman 49 A12
Hope under
　Dinmore 14 A4
Horam 10 H6
Horden 37 J13
Horley 10 E3
Horncastle 29 H11
Horndean 9 F12
Horningsham 8 C3
Hornsea 33 K13
Horrabridge 3 E13
Horringer 25 J3

Horsey 24 C9
Horsford 24 D6
Horsforth 27 B13
Horsham 10 F2
Horsham St Faith . . 24 D7
Horsted Keynes . . . 10 G4
Horton
　Northants 22 K7
　Som 4 B7
Horton in
　Ribblesdale 31 G14
Horwich 26 D7
Houghton 36 H3
Houghton-le-
　Spring 37 H12
Houghton Regis . . . 16 C5
Hounslow 10 B2
Hove 10 J3
Hoveton 24 D7
Hovingham 33 G8
Howden 28 B6
Howpasley 36 C2
Hoxne 24 H6
Hoylake 26 G3
Hucknall 28 K4
Huddersfield 27 D12
Hugh Town 2 C3
Hulland Ward 21 B13
Hullavington 14 H7
Hullbridge 17 F13
Hulme End 27 K12
Humber Bridge 29 B9
Humberston 29 D11
Humshaugh 37 F8
Hundred House 13 A15
Hungerford 15 K12
Hunmanby 33 G12
Hunstanton 24 A1
Huntford 36 C5
Huntingdon 23 H11
Huntley 14 E6
Huntly 50 C4
Hurlford 39 G9
Hurliness 56 H2
Hurn 8 H6
Hursley 9 D10
Hurstbourne Tarrant . 9 B8
Hurstpierpoint 10 H3
Hurworth-on-Tees . 32 C5
Husbands Bosworth . 22 G5
Husinish 55 F2
Huttoft 29 G14
Hutton 26 C5
Hutton Cranswick . . 33 J12
Hutton-le-Hole 33 E9
Hutton Rudby 32 D6
Huyton 26 F5
Hyde 27 F10
Hynish 42 E1
Hythe
　Hants 9 G9
　Kent 11 F12

I

Ibsey 8 G6
Ibstock 22 D2
Icklingham 25 H2
Idmiston 8 D7
Ilchester 5 A9
Ilderton 37 A9
Ilfracombe 6 G4
Ilkeston 22 A3
Ilkley 32 K3
Illogan 2 G4
Ilminster 4 B7
Immingham 29 C10
Inchnadamph 52 F4
Inchture 45 F14
Ingatestone 17 F11
Ingleton 31 G12
Ingoldmells 29 H14
Ingram 37 A9
Ingrave 17 F11
Inkberrow 15 A9
Innellan 38 C6
Innerleithen 40 K6
Innermessan 34 G2

Insch 50 E5
Instow 6 J3
Inver 53 K10
Inverallochy 50 A9
Inveran 52 J7
Inveraray 44 J2
Inverarity 51 N3
Inverbervie 51 K7
Invergarry 48 H4
Invergordon 49 B8
Invergowrie 51 P2
Inverie 47 L7
Inverinate 47 J9
Inverkeilor 51 M5
Inverkeithing 40 E4
Inverkirkaig 52 F2
Inverlochlarig 44 H6
Invermoriston 48 G5
Inverness 48 D7
Inversnaid 44 J5
Inverurie 50 E6
Ipswich 25 L6
Irchester 23 J8
Irlam 27 F8
Ironbridge 20 F7
Irthlingborough . . . 23 H8
Irvine 39 G8
Isbister 57 C4
Isleham 25 H1
Isle of Whithorn . . 34 K5
Islington 10 A4
Islip 15 E14
Ivinghoe 16 D4
Ivybridge 3 F14
Iwerne Minster 8 F3
Ixworth 25 H4

J

Jamestown 39 B8
Jarrow 37 G12
Jaywick 25 P6
Jedburgh 36 A5
John o' Groats 53 A15
Johnshaven 51 L7
Johnston 12 F3
Johnstone 39 D9

K

Kames 38 C4
Kea 2 G5
Kearvaig 52 A4
Kedington 17 A11
Keelby 29 C10
Keele 21 B9
Kegworth 22 C3
Keighley 27 A11
Keillmore 38 B1
Keiss 53 B15
Keith 50 B3
Keld 31 D14
Kellas 49 C12
Kelsale 25 J8
Kelsall 26 J6
Kelso 41 K10
Keltneyburn 45 E9
Kelty 40 D4
Kelvedon 17 D13
Kelynack 2 J1
Kemble 15 G9
Kemnay 50 E6
Kempsey 14 B7
Kempston 16 A5
Kemsing 10 D6
Kendal 31 E11
Kenilworth 22 H1
Kenmore 45 E9
Kennacraig 38 D3
Kennethmont 50 E4
Kennford 4 E3
Kenninghall 24 G5
Kennington 15 F14
Kensington &
　Chelsea 10 B3
Kentford 25 J2
Kentisbeare 4 C4

Kerry 20 H2
Kerrysdale 46 D8
Kershopefoot 36 E3
Kesgrave 25 L7
Kessingland 24 G10
Keswick 31 B8
Kettering 22 H7
Kettletoft 56 C6
Kettlewell 32 G1
Ketton 23 E8
Kew Bridge 10 B3
Kexby 28 F7
Keyingham 29 B11
Keymer 10 H4
Keynsham 14 K5
Keysoe 23 J9
Keyworth 22 B5
Kibworth
　Beauchamp 22 F5
Kidderminster 21 J9
Kidlington 15 E14
Kidsgrove 21 A9
Kidstones 32 F1
Kidwelly 12 F8
Kielder 36 D5
Kilberry 38 D2
Kilbirnie 39 E8
Kilcadzow 39 F13
Kilchattan 38 E6
Kilchenzie 38 H1
Kilchiaran 43 M4
Kilchoan 42 B6
Kilchrenan 44 G2
Kilcreggan 38 B7
Kildonan 53 F11
Kilfinan 38 C4
Kilham 33 H12
Kilkhampton 3 A10
Killamarsh 28 F3
Killean 38 F1
Killearn 39 B10
Killin 44 F7
Killinghall 32 J4
Kilmacolm 39 D8
Kilmaluag 46 D4
Kilmany 40 A6
Kilmarnock 39 G9
Kilmartin 38 A3
Kilmaurs 39 F9
Kilmelford 42 G10
Kilmore 42 F10
Kilmory
　Argyll 38 C2
　Highland 42 A4
　Highland 47 L3
Kilmuir 49 A8
Kilninver 42 F10
Kilnsea 29 C13
Kilrenny 41 E14
Kilsby 22 H4
Kilsyth 39 C12
Kilwinning 38 F7
Kimbolton 23 J9
Kimpton 16 D6
Kinbrace 53 F10
Kinbuck 45 J10
Kincardine
　Fife 40 E2
　Highland 52 K8
Kincardine Bridge . 40 E2
Kincraig 49 H9
Kineton 15 A12
Kingarth 38 E5
Kinghorn 40 E5
Kingsbarns 41 B8
Kingsbridge 4 J1
Kingsbury 21 G13
Kingsclere 9 B10
King's Cliffe 23 F9
Kingsdown 11 E14
Kingskerswell 4 G2
Kingsland 20 K5
Kings Langley 16 E5
Kingsley
　Hants 9 D12
　Staffs 21 B11
King's Lynn 24 D1
King's Somborne . . 9 D8
King's Sutton 15 C14

Kingsteignton 4 F2
King's Thorn 14 C4
Kingston
  Devon 3 G14
  London 10 C2
Kingston Bagpuize .15 G13
Kingston upon Hull . . 29 B9
Kingswear 4 J2
Kingswood 14 J5
King's Worthy 9 D10
Kington 14 A2
Kingussie 49 H8
Kinloch
  Highland 47 M4
  Highland 52 E5
Kinlochbervie 52 C4
Kinlocheil 47 N9
Kinlochewe 46 E10
Kinlochleven 44 C3
Kinlochmoidart 42 A9
Kinloch Rannoch . . 45 D8
Kinloss 49 B11
Kinmel Bay 18 C9
Kinross 40 C4
Kintessack 49 C10
Kintore 50 F6
Kinuachdrachd 43 J9
Kinver 21 H9
Kippax 28 A3
Kippen 39 A11
Kirkabister 57 J5
Kirkbean 35 H10
Kirkbride 35 H13
Kirkburton 27 D12
Kirkby 26 F5
Kirkby-in-Ashfield . . 28 J4
Kirkby-in-Furness . . 31 F8
Kirkby Lonsdale . . 31 G12
Kirkby Malzeard . . 32 G4
Kirkbymoorside . . 33 F8
Kirkby Stephen . . . 31 D13
Kirkby Thore 31 B12
Kirkcaldy 40 D5
Kirkcolm 34 G1
Kirkconnel 35 B8
Kirkcowan 34 G4
Kirkcudbright 34 H8
Kirkham 26 B5
Kirkinner 34 H5
Kirkintilloch 39 C11
Kirkland 35 D9
Kirkliston 40 F4
Kirkmichael
  Perth 45 C12
  S Ayrs 34 C4
Kirk Michael 30 F3
Kirknewton 41 K12
Kirkoswald
  Cumb 36 J4
  S Ayrs 34 C3
Kirkpatrick Durham . 35 F8
Kirkpatrick Fleming 35 F13
Kirkton of Glenisla .45 C10
Kirkton of Largo . . 40 C7
Kirkwall 56 E4
Kirkwhelpington . . . 37 E9
Kirriemuir 51 M2
Kirtling 25 K1
Kirtlington 15 D14
Kirton 23 B11
Kirton in Lindsey . . 29 E8
Knaresborough . . 32 J5
Knayton 32 F6
Knebworth 16 D7
Knighton 20 J3
Knott End-on-Sea . 31 K9
Knottingley 28 B3
Knowle 21 J12
Knutsford 27 H8
Kyleakin 47 J7
Kyle of Lochalsh . . 47 J7
Kylerhea 47 J7
Kylestrome 52 E4

L

Laceby 29 D11
Lacock 15 K8
Ladock 2 G6
Ladybank 40 B6
Lagg
  Argyll 43 L7
  N Ayrs 38 H4
Laggan
  Highland 48 J4
  Highland 48 J7
  Moray 50 D2
Laide 46 B9
Lairg 52 H7
Lakenheath 24 G2
Lamberhurst 10 F7
Lambeth 10 B4
Lambley 36 H5
Lambourn 15 J12
Lamlash 38 G5
Lampeter 13 B9
Lanark 39 F13
Lancaster 31 H10
Lanchester 37 J10
Lancing 10 J2
Landkey 6 J4
Landrake 3 F11
Langford Budville . . 7 J12
Langham 22 D7
Langholm 36 E2
Langport 7 J13
Langsett 27 E13
Langtoft
  E Yorks 33 H12
  Lincs 23 D10
Langton Matravers . 8 K4
Langtree 6 K3
Langwathby 31 A11
Langwell 52 H8
Lanivet 3 E8
Lapford 4 C1
Larbert 39 B13
Largs 38 E7
Larkhall 39 E12
Larkhill 8 C6
Lasswade 40 G6
Latchingdon 17 E13
Latheron 53 E14
Lauder 41 J8
Laugharne 12 E6
Launceston 3 C11
Laurencekirk 51 K6
Laurieston 34 G7
Lavendon 23 K8
Lavenham 25 L4
Lawers 45 F8
Laxey 30 G4
Laxfield 25 H7
Laxford Bridge . . . 52 D4
Laxton 28 H6
Layer de la Haye . . 25 P4
Lazonby 36 J4
Lea 29 F9
Leadburn 40 H5
Leadenham 29 J8
Leaden Roding . . 17 D11
Leadgate 37 H10
Leadhills 35 B9
Leasingham 29 K9
Leatherhead 10 D2
Lechlade-on-
  Thames 15 G11
Ledbury 14 C6
Ledmore 52 G4
Leeds 27 B13
Leedstown 2 H3
Leek 27 K10
Leeming Bar 32 E14
Lee-on-the-Solent . 9 H10
Legbourne 29 F12
Leicester 22 E4
Leigh
  Grt Manchester . . 26 E7
  Worcs 14 A6
Leighton Buzzard . 16 C4
Leintwardine 20 J5
Leiston 25 J9

Leith 40 F5
Leitholm 41 J10
Lelant 2 H3
Lendalfoot 34 D2
Lenham 11 D10
Lennoxtown 39 C11
Leominster 14 A3
Lephin 46 G1
Le Planel . . . . . 4 Guern
Lerwick 57 H5
Lesbury 37 B11
Leslie 40 C5
Lesmahagow . . . 39 F13
Leswalt 34 G1
Letchworth 16 B7
Lettan 56 B7
Letterston 12 D3
Lettoch 49 E12
Leuchars 40 A7
Leumrabhagh . . . 55 F5
Leven
  E Yorks 33 K13
  Fife 40 C6
Leverburgh / An t-
  Ob 55 J2
Lewes 10 J5
Lewisham 10 B4
Lewiston 48 F6
Leyburn 32 E3
Leyland 26 C6
Leysdown-on-Sea . 11 C11
Lhanbryde 49 B13
Liatrie 48 E3
Lichfield 21 F12
Lidgate 25 K2
Lifton 3 C11
Lilleshall 21 E8
Lincoln 29 G8
Lindale 31 F10
Lingfield 10 E4
Linkinhorne 3 D11
Linksness 56 F7
Linlithgow 40 F2
Linslade 16 C4
Linton 17 A10
Liphook 9 E13
Liskeard 3 E10
Liss 9 E12
Lissett 33 J13
Litcham 24 D3
Litherland 26 F4
Littleborough . . . 27 D10
Littlehampton 10 J1
Littlemill 49 C10
Littleport 23 G14
Little Shelford . . . 23 K13
Littlestone-on-Sea 11 G11
Little Stukeley . . . 23 H11
Little Walsingham . 24 B4
Liverpool 26 G4
Liverpool Airport . . 26 G5
Livingston 40 G3
Lizard 2 K4
Llanaber 19 J5
Llanaelhaiarn . . . 18 F3
Llanafan-fawr . . . 19 Q9
Llanarmon 26 K2
Llanarmon Dyffryn
  Ceiriog 20 C2
Llanarth 19 Q4
Llanarthne 13 E9
Llanbadarn Fynydd . 20 J2
Llanbedr 18 H5
Llanbedrog 18 G3
Llanberis 18 E5
Llanbister 20 J2
Llanbrynmair 19 K9
Llanddewi-Brefi . . 19 Q6
Llanddulas 18 C8
Llandeilo 13 D10
Llandinam 19 M10
Llandissilio 12 D5
Llandogo 14 F4
Llandovery 13 C11
Llandrillo 18 G10
Llandrindod Wells . 19 P10
Llandudno 18 B7
Llandybie 13 E10
Llandyfriog 12 B7

Llandygwydd 12 B6
Llandyrnog 26 J2
Llandysul 12 B8
Llanelidan 20 B1
Llanelli 13 F9
Llanelltyd 19 J7
Llanenddwyn 18 H5
Llanerchymedd . . 18 B4
Llanerfyl 19 K10
Llanfaethlu 18 B3
Llanfair Caereinion . 20 F2
Llanfairfechan . . . 18 C6
Llanfairpwllgwngyll .18 C5
Llanfair Talhaiarn . 18 C6
Llanfechain 20 E2
Llanfechell 18 B3
Llan Ffestiniog . . . 18 F7
Llanfihangel-ar-arth 13 C8
Llanfrynach 13 D14
Llanfyllin 20 E2
Llangadfan 19 J10
Llangadog 13 D11
Llangammarch
  Wells 13 B13
Llangefni 18 C4
Llangeitho 19 Q6
Llangelynin 19 K5
Llangennech 13 F9
Llangernyw 18 D8
Llanglydwen 12 D5
Llangoed 18 B4
Llangollen 20 B3
Llangorse 13 D15
Llangranog 12 A7
Llangunllo 20 J3
Llangurig 19 N9
Llangwm 14 F3
Llangybi 19 Q6
Llangynidr 13 E15
Llangynog 18 H10
Llanharan 7 C9
Llanidloes 19 M9
Llanilar 19 N6
Llanllyfni 18 E4
Llannor 18 G3
Llanon 19 P5
Llanpumsaint 12 D8
Llanrhaeadr-ym-
  Mochnant 20 D2
Llanrhian 12 C2
Llanrhidian 13 G8
Llanrhystyd 19 N5
Llanrug 18 D5
Llanrwst 18 D7
Llansannan 18 D9
Llansawel 13 C10
Llanstephan 12 E7
Llanthony 14 D1
Llantrisant 7 C9
Llantwit-Major . . 13 K13
Llanuwchllyn 18 G8
Llanvihangel
  Crucorney 14 D2
Llanwddyn 19 J10
Llanwenog 13 B8
Llanwrda 13 C11
Llanwrtyd Wells . . 13 B12
Llanybydder 13 B9
Llanymynech 20 D3
Llanystumdwy . . 18 G4
Llay 20 A4
Lledrod 19 N6
Llithfaen 18 F3
Llwyngwril 19 J6
Llyswen 13 C15
Loanhead 40 G5
Lochailort 47 N7
Lochaline 42 D8
Lochans 34 H1
Locharbriggs . . . 35 E10
Lochawe 44 A4
Loch Baghasdail /
  Lochboisdale . . 54 H4
Lochboisdale / Loch
  Baghasdail . . . 54 H4
Lochcarron 46 G9
Loch Choire Lodge . 52 E8
Lochdon 42 E9

Lochearnhead 44 G7
Loch Euphoirt 54 C5
Lochgair 38 A4
Lochgelly 40 D4
Lochgilphead 38 B3
Lochgoilhead 44 J4
Lochinver 52 F2
Lochmaben 35 E11
Lochmaddy / Loch nam
  Madadh 54 C6
Loch nam Madadh /
  Lochmaddy 54 C6
Loch Sgioport 54 F5
Lochwinnoch 39 D8
Lockerbie 35 E12
Lockton 33 E10
Loddiswell 4 J1
Loddon 24 F8
Loftus 33 C9
Logan 34 A7
London 10 B4
London Colney . . 16 E6
Long Ashton 14 K4
Long Bennington . . 22 A7
Longbenton 37 G11
Longbridge Deverill . 8 C3
Long Clawson . . . 22 C6
Long Compton . . 15 C11
Long Crendon . . . 16 E1
Longden 14 C7
Long Eaton 22 B3
Longford 14 D7
Longforgan 51 P2
Longformacus . . 41 H10
Longframlington . . 37 C10
Longhope 56 G3
Longhorsley 37 D10
Longhoughton . . 37 B11
Long Itchington . . 22 J3
Long Melford . . . 25 L3
Longnor 27 J11
Long Preston . . . 31 J14
Longridge 26 B7
Longside 50 C9
Long Stratton . . . 24 F6
Long Sutton 23 C13
Longtown
  Cumb 36 G2
  Hereford 14 D2
Loose 11 D8
Lossiemouth . . . 49 A13
Lostock Gralam . . 26 H8
Lostwithiel 3 F8
Loth 56 C6
Loughborough . . 22 C4
Loughor 13 G9
Loughton 17 F9
Louth 29 F12
Lowdham 22 A5
Lower Beeding . . 10 G3
Lower Killeyan . . 43 P4
Lower Langford . . . 7 F13
Lower Mayland . . 17 E14
Lower Shiplake . . 16 H2
Lowestoft 24 F10
Lowick 41 J13
Loxwood 10 F1
Lubcroy 52 H5
Lucker 41 K14
Ludborough 29 E11
Ludford 29 F10
Ludgershall 8 B7
Ludgvan 2 H2
Ludham 24 D8
Ludlow 20 J6
Lugton 39 E9
Lugwardine 14 B4
Lumphanan 50 G4
Lumsden 50 E3
Luss 39 A8
Lusta 46 F2
Luton 16 C5
Lutterworth 22 G4
Lutton 23 G10
Lybster 53 E14

Lydd...........11 H11
Lydd on Sea.......11 H11
Lydford..........3 C13
Lydham..........20 G4
Lydney..........14 F5
Lyme Regis........4 D7
Lyminge.........11 E12
Lymington.........9 H8
Lymm...........26 G7
Lympne.........11 F12
Lympstone........4 E3
Lyndhurst.........8 G7
Lyneham.........15 J9
Lyness..........56 G3
Lynmouth.........6 G6
Lynton..........6 G6
Lytchett Minster.....8 H4
Lytham St Anne's....26 C4
Lythe..........33 C10

M

Mablethorpe......29 F13
Macclesfield......27 H10
Macduff.........50 A5
Machen..........7 C11
Machrihanish......38 H1
Machynlleth......19 K7
Macmerry........40 F7
Madeley.........21 B8
Madley..........14 C3
Maentwrog.......18 G6
Maesteg.........13 H12
Maghull.........26 E4
Magor..........14 H3
Maiden Bradley.....8 D3
Maidenhead......16 H3
Maiden Newton.....5 D9
Maidstone.......11 D8
Maldon.........17 E13
Malham.........31 H14
Mallaig.........47 M6
Mallwyd.........19 J8
Malmesbury......15 H8
Malpas.........20 B6
Maltby.........28 E4
Maltby le Marsh....29 F13
Malton.........33 G9
Manafon.........20 F2
Manby..........29 F13
Manchester.......27 F9
Manchester Airport..27 G9
Manea..........23 G13
Mangotsfield......14 J5
Manningtree......25 M6
Manorbier.......12 G4
Mansfield........28 H4
Mansfield
  Woodhouse......28 H4
Manton.........22 E7
Marazion........2 J3
Marbhig.........55 F6
March..........23 F13
Marden
  Hereford.......14 B4
  Kent.........11 E8
Mareham le Fen...29 H11
Maresfield.......10 G5
Marfleet........29 B10
Margam.........13 H11
Margate.........11 C14
Marham.........24 D2
Market Bosworth...22 E3
Market Deeping....23 D10
Market Drayton....20 C7
Market Harborough..22 G6
Market Lavington....8 B5
Market Rasen.....29 F10
Market Warsop....28 H4
Market Weighton...33 K10
Markfield........22 D3
Markinch........40 C6
Marks Tey.......25 N4
Markyate........16 D5

Marlborough
  Devon..........4 K1
  Wilts..........15 K10
Marlow.........16 G3
Marnhull........5 B11
Marple.........27 G10
Marshchapel......29 E12
Marshfield.......14 J6
Marske-by-the-Sea..33 B8
Marston Magna.....5 A9
Martham.........24 D9
Martin..........8 F5
Martley.........21 K8
Martock.........5 B8
Marton.........28 F7
Marykirk........51 L5
Marypark........49 E12
Maryport........35 K11
Mary Tavy.......3 D13
Marywell
  Aberds.........51 H4
  Angus.........51 N5
Masham.........32 F4
Mathry.........12 C2
Matlock.........28 H1
Mattishall.......24 D5
Mauchline.......39 H9
Maud..........50 C8
Maughold........30 F4
Mawgan.........2 J5
Mawnan.........2 J5
Maxwellheugh.....41 K10
Maybole.........34 C4
Mayfield
  E Sus.........10 G6
  Staffs.........21 B12
Mealabost.......55 D6
Mealsgate.......35 J13
Measham.........22 D2
Medstead........9 D11
Meidrim........12 E6
Meifod.........20 E2
Meigle.........51 N1
Melbourn........17 A8
Melbourne.......22 C2
Melgarve........48 J5
Melksham........8 A4
Mellon Charles....46 B8
Mellor.........26 B7
Melmerby........36 K5
Melrose.........41 K8
Melsonby........32 D3
Meltham........27 D12
Melton.........25 K7
Melton Constable..24 B5
Melton Mowbray...22 D6
Melvaig........46 C7
Melvich........53 B10
Menai Bridge.....18 C5
Mendlesham......25 J6
Mennock........35 C9
Menston........27 A12
Menstrie........39 A13
Meonstoke.......9 F11
Meopham........17 J11
Mere..........8 D3
Mere Brow.......26 D5
Meriden.........21 H13
Merriott........5 B8
Merthyr Tydfil....13 F14
Merton.........10 C3
Meshaw.........6 K6
Messingham......28 D7
Metfield........24 G7
Metheringham....29 H9
Methil.........40 C6
Methlick........50 D7
Methven.........45 G12
Methwold........24 F2
Mevagissey......3 G8
Mexborough......28 D3
Mey..........53 A14
Micheldever......9 D11
Michelmersh......9 E8
Mickleover......22 B2
Mickleton
  Durham.........32 B1
  Glos.........15 B10
Midbea.........56 B4

Middle Barton.....15 D13
Middleham.......32 F3
Middlemarsh......5 C10
Middlesbrough....32 B7
Middleton
  Argyll.........42 D1
  Grt Manchester...27 E9
  Norf.........24 D1
Middleton Cheney..15 B14
Middleton-in-
  Teesdale.......32 B1
Middleton-on-Sea..9 H14
Middleton on the
  Wolds.........33 K11
Middlewich......26 J8
Middlezoy.......7 H12
Midhurst........9 E13
Mid Lavant......9 G13
Midsomer Norton....8 B1
Mid Yell.........57 C6
Milborne Port.....5 B10
Mildenhall......24 H2
Milford.........9 C14
Milford Haven....12 F2
Milford on Sea....8 H7
Millbrook.......3 F12
Millom.........30 F7
Millport........38 E6
Milnathort......40 C4
Milngavie.......39 C10
Milnthorpe......31 F11
Milovaig........46 F1
Milton.........48 C4
Milton Abbot.....3 D11
Milton Keynes....16 B3
Milverton.......7 J10
Minchinhampton...14 G7
Minehead........7 G8
Minera.........20 A3
Minety.........15 H9
Minnigaff.......34 G5
Minster
  Kent.........11 B10
  Kent.........11 C14
Minsterley......20 F4
Mintlaw........50 C9
Mirfield........27 D13
Misterton
  Notts.........28 E6
  Som.........5 C8
Mistley.........25 M6
Mitcheldean.....14 E5
Mitchel Troy.....14 F3
Modbury........3 F14
Moelfre.........18 B5
Moffat.........35 C11
Mold..........26 J3
Monar Lodge.....48 D3
Moniaive........35 D8
Monifieth.......51 P4
Monikie........51 N4
Monkland.......14 A3
Monkokehampton...3 A13
Monkton........39 H8
Monmouth.......14 E4
Montacute.......5 B8
Montgomery.....20 G3
Montrose........51 M6
Monymusk.......50 F5
Morar..........47 M6
Morchard Bishop....4 C1
Mordiford.......14 C4
Morebattle......36 A6
Morecambe......31 H10
Moretonhampstead...4 E1
Moreton-in-Marsh..15 C11
Morley.........27 C13
Morpeth........37 E11
Mortehoe.......6 E8
Mortimer's Cross...20 K5
Morwenstow......6 K1
Mossley........27 E10
Mostyn.........26 H2
Motcombe.......8 E3
Motherwell......39 E12
Mottisfont......9 E8
Moulton
  Lincs.........23 C12
  Northants.......22 J7

Moulton *continued*
  Suff.........25 J2
Mountain Ash.....7 B9
Mountsorrel......22 D4
Mousehole.......2 J2
Mouswald.......35 F11
Moy..........49 E8
Muchalls........51 H7
Much Dewchurch...14 D3
Much Marcle.....14 C5
Much Wenlock....20 F7
Muir..........49 K11
Muirdrum.......51 P4
Muirhead........39 D12
Muirkirk........39 H12
Muir of Ord.....48 C6
Muker.........32 E1
Mulben.........50 B2
Mullion........2 K4
Mullion Cove.....2 K4
Mundesley......24 B7
Mundford.......24 F3
Munlochy.......48 C7
Murlaggan......47 M10
Murton.........37 J13
Musbury........4 D6
Musselburgh.....40 F6
Muthill.........45 H10
Mybster........53 C13
Myddle.........20 D5
Mydroilyn......19 Q4
Mynydd Isa......26 J3

N

Nafferton.......33 J12
Nailsea.........7 D13
Nailsworth......14 G7
Nairn.........49 C9
Nannerch.......26 H2
Nantwich.......20 A7
Nappa.........31 J14
Narberth........12 E5
Narborough......22 F4
Naseby.........22 H5
Navenby........29 J8
Neap..........57 G6
Neath.........13 G11
Necton.........24 E3
Needham Market...25 K5
Needingworth.....23 H12
Nefyn.........18 G3
Neilston........39 E9
Nelson.........27 B9
Nenthead.......36 J6
Neston.........26 H3
Netheravon......8 A2
Netherbury......5 D8
Netherby
Nether Stowey....7 H10
Netherton......37 C8
Nethy Bridge....49 F11
Netley.........9 G9
Nettlebed.......16 G2
Nettleham......29 G9
Nettleton.......29 E10
Nevern.........12 C4
New Abbey......35 G10
New Aberdour....50 A7
New Alresford....9 D11
Newark-on-Trent...28 J7
Newbiggin-by-the-
  Sea.........37 E12
Newbigging......40 J3
Newborough.....18 D4
Newbridge.......7 B11
Newbridge on Wye..19 Q10
Newbrough......36 G7
New Buckenham...24 F5
Newburgh
  Aberds.........50 E8
  Fife.........40 B5
Newburn........37 G10
Newbury........15 K13
Newby Bridge....31 F9
Newbyth........50 B7
Newcastle.......20 H3
Newcastle Emlyn...12 C7
Newcastleton....36 E3

Newcastle-under-
  Lyme.........21 B9
Newcastle-upon-
  Tyne.........37 G11
Newchurch......14 A1
New Costessey....24 D6
New Cumnock.....34 B7
New Deer.......50 C7
Newdigate.......10 E2
New Earswick....33 J8
New Edlington....28 E4
Newent.........14 D6
Newgale........12 D2
New Galloway....34 F7
Newham........10 A5
Newhaven.......10 J5
New Holland....29 B9
Newick........10 G5
Newington
  Kent.........11 C9
  Kent.........11 F12
Newlot.........56 E5
New Luce.......34 G2
Newlyn.........2 J2
Newmachar......50 E7
Newmarket
  Suff.........25 J1
  W Isles.......55 D6
Newmill........50 B3
New Mills.......27 G11
Newmilns.......39 G10
New Milton......8 H7
Newnham.......14 E5
New Pitsligo.....50 B7
Newport
  Essex.........17 B10
  IoW.........9 J10
Newport.......7 C12
  Pembs.........12 C4
  Telford.......21 D8
Newport-on-Tay...40 A7
Newport Pagnell...16 A3
Newquay........2 E5
New Quay.......19 Q3
New Radnor.....20 K3
New Romney.....11 G11
New Rossington...28 E5
New Scone.......45 G13
Newton.........31 J13
Newton Abbot.....4 F2
Newton Arlosh....35 H12
Newton Aycliffe....32 B4
Newton Ferrers....3 G8
Newtongrange....40 G6
Newtonhill......51 H8
Newton le Willows..26 F6
Newton Mearns....39 E10
Newtonmore.....49 J8
Newton Poppleford..4 E4
Newton St Cyres....4 D2
Newton Stewart....34 G5
Newtown
  Hants.........8 G7
  Hereford.......14 B5
  Powys.........20 G2
Newtown St
  Boswells......41 K8
New Tredegar....7 A10
New Waltham.....29 D11
Neyland........12 F3
Ninfield........11 H8
Niton.........9 K10
Nordelph.......23 E14
Norham........41 J9
Normanby le Wold..29 E10
Normanton......28 B3
Northallerton....32 E5
Northam........6 J3
Northampton.....22 J6
North Baddesley....9 F8
North Berwick....41 E8
North Cerney....15 F9
Northchapel......9 E14
North Charlton...37 A10
North Elmham....24 C4
North Ferriby....29 B8
Northfleet......17 H11
North Frodingham..33 J12
North Hill......3 D10

North Hykeham 29 H8	Otter Ferry.........38 B4	Pensilva 3 E10	Portknockie........50 A3	
Northiam 11 G9	Otterton............4 E4	Pentraeth........18 C5	Portlethen........51 H8	
North Kessock 48 D7	Ottery St Mary 4 D4	Pentrefoelas......18 E8	Port Logan.......34 J2	**R**
Northleach........15 E10	Oulton............24 F10	Penybont.........20 K2	Portmahomack...53 K11	
North Molton 6 J6	Oulton Broad......24 F10	Penybontfawr.....20 D1	Portnacroish......44 E1	Rackenford 4 B2
North Newbald 29 A8	Oundle...........23 G9	Pen-y-gop........18 F9	Portnahaven......43 N3	Rackheath........24 D7
Northop 26 J3	Ousdale 53 G12	Penygroes	Portnalong.......47 H3	Rackwick.........56 G2
North Petherton 7 H11	Outwell..........23 E14	Carms...........13 E9	Port Nan Giuran...55 D7	Radcliffe.........27 E8
Northpunds 57 K5	Over.............23 H12	Gwyn 18 E4	Port Nan Long....54 B6	Radcliffe-on-Trent..22 B5
North Queensferry...40 E4	Overbister........56 B6	Penysarn.........18 B4	Port Nis.........55 A7	Radlett..........16 F6
Northrepps 24 B7	Overseal.........21 E13	Penzance 2 J2	Porton...........8 D6	Radley..........15 G14
North Somercotes..29 E13	Overstrand........24 B7	Perranporth 2 F5	Portpatrick.......34 H1	Radstock..........8 B1
North Tawton......3 B14	Overton	Perranzabuloe 2 G5	Port Ramsay.....42 D10	Radyr............7 C10
North Thoresby...29 E11	Hants 9 C10	Pershore 15 B8	Portreath.........2 G4	Raglan..........14 F3
North Walsham....24 B7	Wrex 20 B4	Perth............45 G13	Portree..........46 G4	Rainham.........11 C9
Northwich.........26 H7	Over Wallop........8 D7	Peterborough 23 F10	Port St Mary.....30 J2	Rainworth........28 J5
North Wingfield....28 H3	Owston Ferry.....28 E7	Peterchurch......14 C2	Portskerra.......53 B10	Rampside........31 H8
Northwold 24 F2	Oxenholme.......31 F11	Peterculter.......50 G7	Portslade-by-Sea...10 J3	Ramsbottom......27 D8
Northwood	Oxford...........15 F14	Peterhead.......50 C10	Portsmouth.......9 H11	Ramsey
IoW 9 H9	Oxnam...........36 B6	Peterlee.........37 J13	Portsoy..........50 A4	Cambs.........23 G11
London 16 F5	Oxted...........10 D4	Petersfield.........9 E12	Port Talbot.......13 H11	Essex..........25 M7
Norton	Oykel Bridge.....52 H5	Petworth..........9 E14	Port William......34 J4	IoM............30 F4
Glos 14 D7		Pevensey.........10 J7	Postbridge........3 D14	Ramseycleuch....35 B13
N Yorks..........33 G9	**P**	Pewsey...........8 B6	Potter Heigham...24 D9	Ramsgate........11 C14
Suff..............25 J4		Pickering.........33 F9	Potterne..........8 B4	Rannoch Station...44 D6
Worcs............14 A7	Pabail 55 D7	Piddletrenthide.....5 D11	Potters Bar......16 E7	Rapness.........56 B5
Norton Fitzwarren...7 J10	Paddock Wood....10 E7	Pidley...........23 H12	Potterspury......16 A2	Ratlinghope......50 A9
Norwich 24 E7	Padiham.........27 B9	Pierowall.........56 B4	Potton...........16 A7	Rattray.........45 E13
Norwick 57 A7	Padstow..........2 D7	Pilling...........31 K10	Poulton-le-Fylde...26 B4	Raunds..........23 H8
Nottingham.......22 B4	Paibeil...........54 C4	Pilton............7 H14	Poundstock........3 B9	Ravenglass.......30 E6
Nuneaton.........22 F2	Paignton..........4 H2	Pinchbeck........23 C11	Powick..........14 A7	Ravenshead.......28 J4
Nunney...........8 C2	Pailton..........22 G3	Pinhoe............4 D3	Poynton.........27 G10	Ravenstonedale...31 D13
Nutley...........10 G5	Painscastle......13 B15	Pinmore Mains...34 D3	Praa Sands........2 J3	Rawcliffe........32 J7
Nybster...........53 B15	Painshawfield....37 H9	Pinwherry.......34 E3	Prees............20 C6	Rawmarsh.......28 E3
	Painswick........14 F7	Pirbright..........9 B14	Preesall.........31 K9	Rawtenstall.......27 C9
O	Paisley...........39 D9	Pirnmill.........38 F3	Presbury.........27 H10	Rayleigh.........17 F13
	Palgrave.........24 H6	Pitlochry........45 D11	Prescot..........26 F5	Reading..........16 H2
Oadby 22 E5	Palnackie........35 H9	Pittenweem......41 C8	Prestbury........15 D8	Reay............53 B11
Oakdale 7 B10	Pangbourne......16 H1	Plean............39 B13	Presteigne.......20 K4	Redbourn.........16 D6
Oakengates 21 E8	Papworth Everard..23 J11	Plockton.........47 H8	Preston	Redbridge........17 G9
Oakham 22 E7	Parkeston........25 M7	Pluckley.........11 E10	Borders........41 H10	Redcar..........33 B8
Oban 42 E10	Parkhurst..........9 H9	Plumpton.........36 K4	Dorset..........5 E10	Red Dial........35 J13
Ochiltree 34 A6	Parracombe 6 G5	Plymouth.........3 F12	E Yorks........29 A10	Redditch.........21 K11
Ockley...........10 F2	Partney..........29 H13	Plympton.........3 F13	Kent...........11 C13	Redesmouth......36 E7
Odie............56 D6	Parton...........30 B5	Plymstock........3 F13	Lancs..........26 B6	Redhill..........10 E3
Odiham..........9 C12	Pateley Bridge....32 H3	Pocklington......33 K10	Preston Candover...9 C11	Red Houses.......5 Jersey
Offord D'Arcy 23 J11	Pathhead.........40 G7	Polegate..........10 J6	Prestonpans 40 F6	Redland..........56 D3
Ogbourne St	Patna............34 B5	Polesworth.......21 F13	Prestwich........27 E9	Redlynch..........8 F7
George 15 J10	Patrick Brompton..32 E4	Polloch..........42 B10	Prestwick........34 A4	Redmile..........22 B7
Okehampton 3 B13	Patrington.......29 B12	Polperro..........3 G9	Prestwood.......16 E3	Redmire.........32 E2
Old Basing........9 B11	Patterdale........31 C9	Polruan...........3 G9	Princes Risborough..16 E3	Red Point........46 E7
Old Bolingbroke...29 H12	Paull............29 B10	Polwarth.........41 H10	Princetown.......3 D13	Redruth..........2 G4
Oldbury..........14 G5	Paulton...........8 B1	Polzeath..........2 D7	Probus..........2 G6	Reedham.........24 E9
Old Colwyn 18 C8	Peacehaven.......10 J5	Pontardawe......13 F11	Prudhoe.........37 G9	Reepham.........24 C5
Old Deer.........50 C8	Peak Forest......27 H12	Pontardulais......13 F9	Pubil............44 E6	Reeth............32 E2
Old Fletton.......23 F10	Peasedown St John..8 B2	Pontefract.......28 B3	Pucklechurch.....14 J5	Reigate..........10 E3
Oldham..........27 E10	Peasenhall........25 J8	Ponteland.......37 F10	Puddletown.......5 D11	Reiss............53 C15
Old Leake........29 K12	Peasmarsh.......11 G10	Ponterwyd.......19 M7	Pudsey..........27 B13	Renfrew.........39 D10
Oldmeldrum......50 E7	Peebles..........40 J5	Pontesbury......20 F5	Pulborough......10 H1	Rennington......37 B11
Old Radnor.......14 A1	Peel.............30 G2	Pontrhydfendigaid..19 P7	Pulham Market....24 G6	Repton..........22 C2
Olgrinmore......53 C12	Pegswood........37 E11	Pontrilas.........14 D3	Pulham St Mary...24 G7	Resolven........13 F12
Ollaberry........57 D4	Peinchorran......47 H5	Pontyates........13 F8	Pumpsaint.......13 B10	Reston..........41 G11
Ollerton.........28 H5	Pembrey..........12 F8	Pontyberem......13 E8	Purfleet.........17 H10	Retford..........28 F6
Olney...........22 K7	Pembridge.......14 A3	Pontypool.........7 A11	Purley	Reydon..........24 H10
Ombersley.......21 K9	Pembroke.........12 F3	Pontypridd........7 C9	London.........10 C4	Rhayader........19 P9
Onchan..........30 H3	Pembroke Dock....12 F3	Pool.............2 G4	W Berks........16 H1	Rhewl...........26 J2
Onich...........44 C2	Pembury.........10 F7	Poole............8 J5	Purton...........15 H9	Rhiconich.......52 C4
Opinan..........46 B8	Penally..........12 G5	Poolewe.........46 D8	Puttenham........9 C14	Rhiw............18 H2
Ordhead.........50 F5	Penarth..........7 D10	Pooley Bridge....31 B10	Pwllheli.........18 G3	Rhondda.........13 G13
Ordie...........50 G3	Pencader........12 C8	Porlock...........6 G7	Pyle............13 H12	Rhoose...........7 E9
Orford...........25 K9	Pencoed........13 H13	Port Appin........44 E1		Rhoslan..........18 F4
Orleton..........20 K6	Pendeen..........2 H1	Port Askaig......43 M6	**Q**	Rhosllanerchrugog..20 B3
Ormesby St	Penderyn........13 F13	Portavadie.......38 C4		Rhosneigr........18 C3
Margaret.......24 D9	Pendine.........12 F6	Port Bannatyne...38 D5	Quadring 23 B11	Rhos-on-Sea......18 B8
Ormiston........40 G7	Penicuik.........40 G5	Port Carlisle.....35 G13	Quainton.........16 D2	Rhossili.........12 H8
Ormskirk........26 D5	Penistone........27 E13	Port Charlotte....43 N4	Quedgeley........14 E7	Rhostryfan.......18 E4
Orpington.......10 C5	Penkridge........21 E10	Port Ellen........43 P5	Queenborough...11 B10	Rhuddlan........18 C10
Orton...........31 D12	Penmachno.......18 F7	Portencross.......38 F6	Queensbury......27 C12	Rhyd-Ddu........18 E5
Osbournby......23 B9	Penmaenmawr....18 C7	Port Erin.........30 J2	Queensferry	Rhyl............18 B10
Oskamull........42 D6	Pennan..........50 A7	Port Eynon.......13 H8	Edin............40 F4	Rhymney........13 F15
Osmotherley.....32 E6	Pennyghael......42 F7	Port Glasgow.....39 C8	Flint............26 J4	Rhynie..........50 E3
Ossett..........27 D13	Penpont.........35 D9	Portgordon.......50 A2	Quorndon........22 D4	Riccall..........28 A5
Oswaldtwistle....27 C8	Penrhyndeudraeth..18 G3	Porth............7 B9		Richmond
Oswestry........20 D3	Penrith..........31 A11	Porthcawl........13 J12		London.........10 B2
Otford..........10 D6	Penryn...........2 H5	Port Henderson...46 D7		N Yorks........32 D3
Othery..........7 H12	Pensford..........8 A1	Porthleven........2 J4		
Otley...........32 K3	Penshaw.........37 H12	Porthmadog......18 G5		
Otterburn........36 D7	Penshurst........10 E6	Port Isaac.........2 D7		
		Portishead.......14 J3		

Rickmansworth 16 F5
Ridsdale 37 E8
Rievaulx 32 F7
Rigside 39 G13
Rillington 33 G10
Ringford 34 H7
Ringmer 10 H5
Ringwood 8 G6
Ripley
　Derbys 28 J3
　N Yorks 32 H4
　Sur 10 D1
Ripon 32 G5
Ripponden 27 C11
Risca 7 C11
Rishton 27 B8
Roade 22 K6
Roadhead 36 F4
Roberton 36 B3
Robertsbridge 11 G8
Robin Hood's Bay . . 33 D11
Rocester 21 C12
Rochdale 27 D9
Roche 2 F7
Rochester
　Medway 17 J12
　Northumb 36 D7
Rochford 17 G13
Rockcliffe
　Cumb 36 G2
　Dumfries 35 H9
Rockingham 22 F7
Rogart 53 H9
Rogate 9 E13
Roghadal 55 J2
Rolvenden 11 F9
Romford 17 G10
Romsey 9 E8
Ropsley 23 B9
Rosedale Abbey 33 E9
Rosehall 52 H6
Rosehearty 50 A8
Rosemarket 12 F3
Rosemarkie 49 C8
Roskhill 46 G2
Roslin 40 G5
Rosneath 38 B7
Ross 41 K14
Rossett 26 K4
Ross-On-Wye 14 D5
Rosyth 40 E4
Rothbury 37 C9
Rotherham 28 E3
Rothes 49 D13
Rothesay 38 D5
Rothienorman 50 D6
Rothiesholm 56 D6
Rothwell
　Northants 22 G7
　W Yorks 28 B2
Rottal 51 K2
Rottingdean 10 J4
Rowanburn 36 F3
Rowlands Gill 37 H10
Roxburgh 41 K10
Roxby 29 C8
Royal Leamington
　Spa 22 J2
Royal Tunbridge
　Wells 10 F6
Roybridge 44 A4
Royston
　Herts 17 A8
　S Yorks 28 D2
Royton 27 E10
Ruabon 20 B4
Ruan Minor 2 K5
Ruardean 14 E5
Rubery 21 J10
Rudston 33 H12
Rufford 26 D5
Rugby 22 H4
Rugeley 21 E11
Ruislip 16 G6
Rumburgh 24 G8
Rumney 7 D11

Runcorn 26 G6
Rushden 23 J8
Rushwick 14 A7
Ruskington 29 J9
Rutherglen 39 D11
Ruthin 26 K2
Ruthven 49 H8
Ruthwell 35 G11
Ryal 37 F9
Rydal 31 D9
Ryde 9 H10
Rye 11 G10
Ryhall 23 D9
Ryhope 37 H13
Ryton 22 H2

S

Sacriston 37 J11
Saddell 38 G2
Saffron Walden 17 B10
Sageston 12 F4
St Abb's 41 G12
St Agnes 2 G5
St Albans 16 E6
St Andrews 41 B8
St Ann's 35 D11
St Arvans 14 G4
St Asaph 18 C10
St Athan 7 E9
St Aubin . . . . 5 Jersey
St Austell 3 F8
St Bees 30 C5
St Blazey 3 F8
St Breward 3 D8
St Briavels 14 F4
St Bride's Major . . . 13 J12
St Buryan 2 J1
St Clears 12 E6
St Columb Major 2 E6
St Columb Minor 2 E6
St Combs 50 A9
St Cyrus 51 L6
St David's 12 D1
St Day 2 G5
St Dennis 2 F7
St Dogmaels 12 B5
St Dominick 3 E11
St Enoder 2 F6
St Erth 2 H3
St Fergus 50 B9
St Fillans 45 G8
St Germans 3 F11
St Harmon 19 N9
St Helens 26 F6
St Helier . . . . 5 Jersey
St Issey 2 D7
St Ives
　Cambs 23 H12
　Corn 2 H3
St John's
　IoM 30 G2
　Jersey . . . . 5 Jersey
St Johns Chapel . . . 31 A14
St John's Town of
　Dalry 34 E7
St Just 2 H1
St Keverne 2 K5
St Leonards 11 J9
St Levan 2 J1
St Mabyn 3 D8
St Margaret's-at-
　Cliffe 11 E14
St Margaret's Hope . 56 G4
St Martin's . . . . 5 Jersey
St Mary Bourne 9 B9
St Mary's 54 F4
St Mary's Bay 11 G11
St Mawes 2 H6
St Mellons 7 D11
St Merryn 2 D6
St Minver 2 D7
St Monance 41 C8
St Neots 23 J10
St Newlyn East 2 F6
St Olaves 24 F9
St Osyth 25 P6
St Ouens . . . . 5 Jersey

St Peter Port . . . . . . 4 Guern
St Peter's . . . . 5 Jersey
St Sampson . . . . . . 4 Guern
St Stephen 2 F7
St Teath 3 D8
St Tudy 3 D8
Salcombe 4 K1
Sale 27 F8
Salen
　Argyll 42 D7
　Highland 42 B8
Salford 27 F9
Salford Priors 15 A9
Saline 40 D3
Salisbury 8 E6
Sallachy 52 H7
Saltash 3 F12
Saltburn-by-the-
　Sea 33 B8
Saltcoats 38 F7
Saltfleet 29 E13
Saltfleetby 29 E13
Saltwood 11 F12
Sampford Courtenay . 3 B14
Sanaigmore 43 L4
Sandbach 27 J8
Sandbank 38 C6
Sandgate 11 F13
Sandhead 34 J2
Sandhurst 16 J3
Sandleigh 15 F13
Sandness 57 G2
Sandown 9 J10
Sandringham 24 B1
Sandwich 11 D14
Sandy 16 A6
Sanquhar 35 B8
Sarnau 12 A7
Sarnesfield 14 A2
Sarre 11 C13
Satterthwaite 31 E9
Saundersfoot 12 F4
Sawbridgeworth 17 D9
Sawston 17 A9
Sawtry 23 G10
Saxilby 29 G8
Saxlingham
　Nethergate 24 F7
Saxmundham 25 J8
Saxthorpe 24 B6
Scalasaig 43 J5
Scalby 33 F12
Scalloway 57 J4
Scalpay 55 H4
Scamblesby 29 G11
Scarborough 33 F12
Scardoy 48 C3
Scarinish 42 D2
Scarning 24 H6
Scole 24 H6
Sconser 47 H5
Scopwick 29 J9
Scorton 32 D4
Scotch Corner 32 D4
Scotter 28 D7
Scourie 52 D3
Scousburgh 57 L4
Scrabster 53 B13
Scremerston 41 J13
Scunthorpe 28 C7
Seaford 10 K5
Seaham 37 J13
Seahouses 41 K15
Seamer 33 F12
Sea Palling 24 C9
Seascale 30 D6
Seaton
　Cumb 30 A6
　Devon 4 E5
Seaton Delaval 37 F12
Seaview 9 H11
Sebergham 31 A4
Sedbergh 31 E12
Sedgefield 32 A5
Seend 8 B4
Selborne 9 D12
Selby 28 A5
Selkirk 36 A3
Sellafield 30 D6

Selsey 9 H13
Sennen 2 J1
Sennybridge 13 D13
Settle 31 H14
Sevenoaks 10 D6
Seven Sisters 13 F12
Severn Beach 14 H4
Severn Stoke 14 B7
Sgarasta Mhor 55 H2
Sgiogarstaigh 55 A7
Shaftesbury 8 E3
Shalcombe 9 J8
Shaldon 4 F3
Shalford 9 C15
Shanklin 9 J10
Shap 31 C11
Sharnbrook 23 J8
Sharpness 14 F5
Shawbury 20 D6
Shawford 9 E9
Shebbear 3 A12
Sheerness 11 B10
Sheffield 28 F2
Shefford 16 B6
Sheigra 52 B3
Shenfield 17 F11
Shepley 27 D12
Shepshed 22 D3
Shepton Mallet 8 C1
Sherborne 5 B10
Sherborne St John . . 9 B13
Sherburn 33 G11
Sherburn in Elmet . . 28 A3
Shere 10 C1
Sherfield English 8 E7
Sherfield on Loddon . 9 B11
Sheriff Hutton 33 H8
Sheringham 24 A6
Sherston 14 H7
Shiel Bridge 47 K9
Shieldaig 46 F8
Shifnal 21 F8
Shilbottle 37 C10
Shildon 32 B4
Shillingstone 8 G3
Shillington 16 B6
Shinfield 16 J2
Shipdham 24 E4
Shipley 27 B12
Shipston-on-Stour . 15 C11
Shipton under
　Wychwood 15 E11
Shirebrook 28 H4
Shoeburyness 17 G14
Shoreham-by-Sea . . 10 J3
Shorwell 9 J9
Shotley Gate 25 M7
Shottermill 9 D13
Shottisham 25 L8
Shotts 39 D13
Shrewsbury 20 E5
Shrewton 8 C5
Shrivenham 15 H11
Siabost 55 C4
Sible Hedingham . . . 25 M2
Sibsey 29 J12
Sidbury 4 E5
Sidford 4 E5
Sidlesham 9 H13
Sidmouth 4 E5
Silloth 35 H12
Silsden 32 K2
Silverdale 31 G10
Silverstone 16 A1
Silverton 4 C3
Simonsbath 6 H6
Singleton 9 F13
Sittingbourne 11 C10
Sixpenny Handley . . . 8 F5
Sizewell 25 J9
Skegness 29 H14
Skellingthorpe 29 G8
Skelmersdale 26 E5
Skelmorlie 38 D6
Skelton
　Cumb 31 A10
　Redcar 33 C8
Skerray 52 B8
Skinburness 35 H12

Skipness 38 E4
Skipsea 33 J13
Skipton 32 J1
Skirlaugh 29 A10
Slaidburn 31 J13
Slaithwaite 27 D11
Slaley 37 H8
Slamannan 39 C13
Sleaford 23 A9
Sledmere 33 H11
Sleights 33 D10
Sligachan 47 H4
Slough 16 H4
Smailholm 41 K9
Smarden 11 E9
Smethwick 21 H11
Smithfield 36 G3
Snainton 33 F11
Snaith 28 B5
Snape 25 K8
Sneaton 33 D10
Snettisham 24 B1
Snodland 17 J12
Soham 23 H14
Solas 54 B5
Solihull 21 H12
Solva 12 D1
Somerby 22 D6
Somercotes 28 J3
Somersham 23 H12
Somerton 7 J13
Sonning 16 H2
Sonning Common . . . 16 H2
Sopley 8 H6
Sorbie 34 J5
Sordale 53 B13
Sorisdale 42 B4
Sorn 39 H10
Sortat 53 B14
Soulby 31 C13
Southam 22 J3
Southampton 9 F9
South Anston 28 F4
South Benfleet 17 G12
Southborough 10 E6
South Brent 3 F14
South Cave 29 A8
South Cerney 15 G9
South Elkington 29 F11
Southend 38 K1
Southend-on-Sea . . 17 G13
Southery 24 F1
South Harting 9 F12
South Hayling 9 H12
South Kelsey 29 E9
South Kirkby 28 C3
Southminster 17 F14
South Molton 6 J5
South Ockendon . . . 17 G10
South Otterington . . . 32 F5
South Petherton 5 B8
South Petherwin . . . 3 C11
Southport 26 D4
South Shields 37 G12
South Tawton 3 B14
South Walsham 24 D8
Southwark 10 B4
South Warnborough . 9 C12
Southwell 28 J5
Southwick 10 J3
Southwold 24 H10
South Woodham
　Ferrers 17 F13
South Wootton 24 C1
South Zeal 3 B14
Sowerby 32 F6
Sowerby Bridge . . . 27 C11
Spalding 23 C11
Spaldwick 23 H10
Sparkford 5 A10
Spean Bridge 44 A4
Speke 26 G5
Spennymoor 32 A4
Spey Bay 50 A2
Spilsby 29 H13
Spittal 12 D3
Spittal of Glenmuick . 51 J1
Spittle of Glenshee . 45 B12
Spixworth 24 D7

Spofforth 32 J5
Spott 41 F9
Sproatley 29 A10
Stadhampton 16 F1
Staffin 46 E4
Stafford 21 D10
Staindrop 32 B3
Staines 16 H5
Stainforth
 N Yorks. 31 H14
 S Yorks. 28 C5
Stainton
 Lincs. 29 G9
 Mbro. 32 C6
Staintondale 33 E11
Staithes 33 C9
Stalbridge 5 B11
Stalham 24 C8
Stallingborough 29 C10
Stalybridge 27 F10
Stamford 23 E9
Stamford Bridge 33 J9
Stamfordham 37 F9
Standish 26 D6
Standlake 15 F12
Stanford le Hope 17 G12
Stanford on Teme 21 K8
Stanhope 37 K8
Stanley
 Durham 37 H11
 Perth 45 F13
Stannington 37 E11
Stansted Airport. . . .17 C10
Stansted
 Mountfitchet 17 C10
Stanton 25 H4
Stanton Harcourt . . .15 F13
Stanton St John 15 F14
Stanway 15 C9
Stanwix 36 H3
Stapleford 22 B3
Staplehurst 11 E8
Starcross 4 F3
Staunton 14 D6
Staunton on Wye 14 B2
Staveley
 Cumb 31 E10
 Derbys 28 G3
Staxigoe 53 C15
Staxton 33 G12
Steeple Bumpstead 17 A11
Steeple Claydon 16 C2
Stein 46 F2
Stenhousemuir 39 B13
Stenness 57 E3
Stevenage 16 C7
Stevenston 38 F7
Stewarton 39 F9
Steyning 10 H2
Stibb Cross 6 K3
Stichill 41 K10
Stickford 29 H12
Stickney 29 J12
Stillington 32 H7
Stilton 23 G10
Stirling 39 A12
Stobbs. 36 C4
Stobo 40 K4
Stock 17 F12
Stockbridge. 9 D8
Stockport. 27 F10
Stocksbridge 27 F13
Stockton 22 J3
Stockton-on-Tees . . .32 B6
Stoer 52 F2
Stoke 11 B9
Stoke Albany 22 G7
Stoke Ferry 24 F2
Stoke Fleming 4 J2
Stoke Gabriel 4 H2
Stoke Mandeville 16 E3
Stokenchurch 16 F2
Stoke-on-Trent 21 B9
Stoke Poges 16 G4
Stoke Prior 21 K10
Stokesley 32 C7
Stone
 Bucks 16 D2
 Glos 14 G5

Stone continued
 Staffs 21 C9
Stonehaven 51 J7
Stonehouse
 Glos 14 F7
 S Lanark 39 F12
Stoneykirk 34 H2
Stonham Aspal 25 K6
Stony Stratford. 16 B3
Stornoway 55 D6
Storrington 10 H1
Stotfold 16 B7
Stourbridge. 21 H10
Stourpaine. 8 G3
Stourport-on-
 Severn 21 J9
Stow 40 J7
Stow Bardolph 24 E1
Stowmarket. 25 K5
Stow-on-the-Wold 15 D11
Strachan. 51 H5
Strachur. 44 J2
Stradbroke. 25 H7
Straiton 34 C4
Stranraer 34 G1
Stratford St Mary . . .25 M5
Stratford-upon-
 Avon 15 A11
Strathan 52 B7
Strathaven 39 F11
Strathblane 39 C10
Strathdon 50 F2
Strathkanaird 52 H3
Strathpeffer. 48 C5
Strathy 53 B10
Strathyre 44 H7
Stratmiglo 40 B5
Stratton
 Corn 3 A10
 Glos 15 F9
Stratton St
 Margaret 15 H10
Streatley 15 J14
Street 7 H13
Strensall 33 H8
Stretford. 27 F9
Stretham 23 H14
Stretton
 Rutland. 23 D8
 Staffs 21 D13
 Warr. 26 G7
Strichen 50 B8
Stromeferry 47 H8
Stromemore 47 H8
Stromness 56 E2
Stronachlachar. 44 H6
Strone 38 B6
Strontian 42 B10
Stroud 14 F7
Struy 48 D4
Stubbington 9 G10
Studland. 8 J5
Studley 21 K11
Sturminster Marshall .8 H4
Sturminster Newton. .5 B11
Sturry 11 D12
Sturton 28 F7
Sudbury
 Derbys 21 C12
 Suff. 25 L3
Sulby 30 F3
Sullom 57 E4
Sully 7 E10
Sumburgh 57 M5
Sunderland 37 H13
Sunk Island 29 C11
Sunninghill 16 J4
Sutterton 23 B11
Sutton
 Cambs 23 H13
 London 10 C3
Sutton Bridge 23 C13
Sutton Coldfield. 21 G12
Sutton Courtenay . . .15 G14
Sutton-in-Ashfield . .28 H3
Sutton Lane Ends. . . .27 H10
Sutton-on-Sea 29 F14
Sutton-on-Trent 28 H6
Sutton Scotney. 9 D9

Sutton-under-
 Whitestonecliffe . . .32 F6
Sutton Valence 11 E9
Swadlincote 21 E13
Swaffham. 24 E3
Swalcliffe. 15 C12
Swalecliffe. 11 C12
Swanage 8 K5
Swanley 10 C6
Swansea. 13 G10
Sway 8 H7
Swindon 15 H10
Swinefleet 28 B6
Swineshead. 23 A11
Swinton
 Borders 41 J11
 Grt Manchester . . .27 E8
 S Yorks 28 E3
Symbister. 57 F6
Symington 40 K2
Symonds Yat 14 E4
Syresham 16 A1
Syston 22 D5

T

Tadcaster 32 K6
Tadley 9 A11
Tain 53 K9
Talgarth 13 C15
Talladale. 48 G3
Talley. 13 C10
Talsarnau 18 G6
Talybont 19 M6
Tal-y-llyn. 19 K7
Talysarn 18 E4
Tamerton Foliot 3 F12
Tamworth. 21 F13
Tangmere. 9 G13
Tannadice 51 M3
Tanworth-in-Arden 21 J12
Taobh Tuath. 55 J1
Tarbert 38 D3
Tarbert / Aird Asaig
 Tairbeart 55 G3
Tarbet
 Argyll 44 J5
 Highland. 47 M7
Tarbolton 39 H9
Tarland 50 G3
Tarleton 26 C5
Tarporley 26 J6
Tarrant Hinton 8 G4
Tarskavaig 47 K5
Tarves 50 D7
Tarvin 26 J5
Tattenhall. 26 K5
Tattersett 24 B3
Taunton 7 J11
Tavistock 3 D12
Tay Bridge 40 A7
Tayinloan 38 F2
Taynuilt 44 F2
Tayport 40 A7
Teangue 47 L6
Tebay 31 D12
Tedburn St Mary 4 D2
Teesside 32 B6
Teignmouth. 4 F3
Telford 20 F7
Temple Combe 5 A11
Temple Ewell 11 E13
Temple Sowerby 31 B12
Templeton 12 E5
Tenbury Wells 20 K7
Tenby 12 G5
Tenterden 11 F9
Terrington 33 G8
Terrington St
 Clement 23 C14
Tetbury 14 G7
Tetney 29 D12
Tetsworth. 16 E1
Teviothead 36 C3
Tewkesbury 15 C8
Teynham 11 C10
Thame. 16 E2
Thatcham. 15 K14

Thaxted 17 B11
Theale. 16 H1
The Barony 56 D2
The Mumbles 13 H10
Thetford 24 G3
Thirsk 32 F6
Thornaby on Tees. . . .32 C6
Thornbury 14 H5
Thorndon 25 J6
Thorne 28 C5
Thorney 23 E11
Thornham 24 A2
Thornhill
 Dumfries 35 D9
 Stirling 45 J8
Thornthwaite 31 B8
Thornton 26 A4
Thornton-le-Dale . . .33 F10
Thorpe 24 E7
Thorpe-le-Soken. . . .25 N6
Thorverton. 4 C3
Thrapston 23 H8
Three Legged Cross . .8 G5
Threlkeld 31 B9
Threshfield 32 H1
Thrumster 53 D15
Thurcroft 28 F3
Thurlby 23 D10
Thurlestone 3 G14
Thurmaston. 22 E5
Thursby 36 H2
Thurso 53 B13
Ticehurst 11 G8
Tickhill 28 E4
Tideswell 27 H12
Tidworth. 8 C7
Tighnabruaich 38 C4
Tilbury 17 H11
Tillicoultry 40 D2
Tillingham 17 E15
Tilmanstone 11 E13
Timberscombe 7 G8
Timsbury 8 B1
Tingewick 16 B1
Tingwall 56 D3
Tintagel 3 C8
Tintern Parva 14 F4
Tipton 21 G10
Tiptree 25 P4
Tisbury 8 E4
Titchfield 9 G10
Tiverton 4 B3
Toab. 58 L4
Tobermory 42 C6
Toberonochy 43 H9
Tobha Mor 54 F4
Toddington 16 C5
Todmorden 27 C10
Tolastadh bho
 Thuath 55 C7
Tollesbury 25 Q4
Tolpuddle 5 D11
Tomatin 49 F9
Tomdoun 48 H2
Tomintoul. 49 G12
Tomnavoulin 49 F13
Tonbridge 10 E6
Tondu 13 H12
Tong 21 F9
Tongue 52 C7
Tonyrefail. 7 C9
Topcliffe. 32 G6
Topsham 4 E3
Torbay 4 H3
Torcross 4 J2
Torness 48 F6
Torphins 50 G5
Torpoint 3 F12
Torquay. 4 G3
Torridon 46 F9
Torroble 52 H7
Torthorwald. 35 E11
Torver 31 E8
Toscaig. 47 H7
Totland 9 J8
Totley 28 F2
Totnes 4 H1
Totton 9 F8
Towcester 16 A2

Tower Hamlets 10 A4
Tow Law 37 K10
Town Yetholm 36 A7
Trafford Park. 27 F8
Tranent 40 F7
Trawsfynydd 18 G7
Trecastle. 13 D12
Tredegar. 13 F15
Trefeglwys 19 L9
Trefnant 18 C10
Trefriw 18 D7
Tregaron. 19 Q6
Tregony 2 G7
Tregynon 20 G2
Treharris. 7 B10
Trelech 12 C6
Tremadog. 18 G5
Trenance 2 E6
Trentham 21 B9
Treorchy 13 G13
Tresilian 2 G6
Tretower. 13 D15
Treuddyn 26 K3
Trimdon 32 A5
Trimley 25 M7
Tring 16 D4
Trinity . . . . .5 Jersey
Troon 39 G8
Troutbeck. 31 D10
Trowbridge 8 B3
Trull 7 J11
Trumpan. 46 E2
Trumpington 23 K13
Trunch. 24 B7
Truro 2 G6
Tuddenham 25 H2
Tudweiliog. 18 G2
Tullynessle. 50 F4
Tummel Bridge. 45 D9
Tunstall. 25 K8
Turnberry. 34 C3
Turriff 50 B6
Turvey. 23 K8
Tutbury 21 D13
Tuxford 28 G6
Twatt 56 D2
Tweedmouth. 41 H12
Tweedshaws 35 B11
Tweedsmuir. 35 A11
Twenty 23 C10
Twyford
 Hants 9 E9
 Leics. 22 D6
 Wokingham 16 H3
Tydd St Giles 23 D13
Tydd St Mary 23 D13
Tylorstown. 7 B9
Tyndrum 44 F5
Tynemouth. 37 G12
Ty'n-y-groes. 18 C7
Tywardreath 3 F8
Tywyn 19 K5

U

Uckfield 10 G5
Uddingston 39 D11
Uffculme 4 B4
Uffington 15 H12
Ufford 25 K8
Ugborough 3 F14
Uig. 46 E4
Ulbster 53 D15
Ulceby 29 C9
Ulceby Cross 29 G13
Uley 14 G6
Ullapool 52 J3
Ulsta 57 D5
Ulverston 31 G8
Unapool 52 E4
Upavon 8 B6
Upchurch 7 J12
Upper Chapel 13 C14
Upper Heyford 15 D14
Upper Hindhope. 36 C6

Upper Poppleton 32 J7
Upper Tean 21 C11
Uppertown 56 G4
Uppingham 22 F7
Upton 26 J5
Upton Snodsbury ... 15 A8
Upton upon Severn . 14 B7
Upwey 5 E10
Urchfont 8 B5
Urmston 27 F8
Usk 14 F2
Usselby 29 E9
Uttoxeter 21 C11
Uyeasound 57 B6

V

Valley 18 C2
Veness 56 C5
Ventnor 9 K10
Verwood 8 G5
Veryan 2 H7
Vickerstown 30 H7
Vidlin 57 F5
Virginia Water 16 J5
Voe 57 F5
Voy 56 E2

W

Waddesdon 16 D2
Waddingham 29 E8
Waddington 29 H8
Wadebridge 2 D7
Wadhurst 10 F7
Wainfleet All
  Saints 29 H13
Wakefield 28 B2
Walberswick 25 H9
Walcott 29 J10
Walderslade 17 J12
Waldron 10 H6
Walford 20 J4
Walkerburn 40 K6
Walkeringham 28 E6
Wallasey 26 F4
Wallingford 16 G1
Walls 57 H3
Wallsend 37 G12
Walmer 11 E14
Walpole 23 D13
Walsall 21 G11
Walsham le Willows . 25 H4
Walsoken 23 D13
Waltham 29 D11
Waltham Abbey 17 F8
Waltham Forest 17 G8
Waltham on the
  Wolds 22 C7
Walton 36 G4
Walton-on-Thames . 10 C2
Walton-on-the-
  Naze 25 N7
Wanborough 15 H11
Wandsworth 10 B3
Wangford 24 H9
Wansford 23 F9
Wantage 15 H13
Warboys 23 G12
Wardington 15 B13
Wardle 26 K7
Ware 17 D8
Wareham 8 J4
Wargrave 16 H2
Wark 36 F7
Warkworth 37 C11
Warley 21 H11
Warminster 8 C3
Warrington 26 G7
Warton 31 G10
Warwick 22 J1
Wasbister 56 C3

Washaway 3 E8
Washford 7 H9
Washingborough ... 29 G9
Washington
  T&W 37 H12
  W Sus 10 H2
Watchet 7 G9
Watchfield 15 G11
Waterbeach 23 J13
Waterhead 51 K3
Waterhouses 21 A11
Wateringbury 10 D7
Waterlooville 9 G11
Watford 16 F6
Wath upon Dearne . 28 E3
Watlington
  Norf 24 D1
  Oxon 16 F1
Watten 53 C14
Watton 24 E4
Waunfawr 18 E5
Weachyburn 50 B5
Wearhead 36 K7
Weasenham 24 C3
Weaverham 26 H7
Weaverthorpe 33 G11
Wedmore 7 G13
Wednesbury 21 G10
Wednesfield 21 F10
Weedon Bec 22 J5
Weeley 25 N6
Welbourn 29 J8
Weldon
  Northants 23 G8
  Northumb 37 D10
Welford
  Northants 22 G5
  W Berks 15 J13
Wellesbourne 15 A11
Wellingborough ... 22 J7
Wellington
  Som 4 B5
  Telford 20 E7
Wells 7 G14
Wells-next-the-Sea . 24 A4
Welney 23 F14
Welshampton 20 C5
Welshpool 20 F3
Welton 29 G9
Welwyn Garden City . 16 D7
Wem 20 D6
Wembury 3 G13
Wemyss Bay 38 C6
Wendover 16 E3
Wensley 32 E3
Wenvoe 7 D10
Weobley 14 A3
Werrington 3 C11
West Bergholt 25 N4
Westbourne 9 G12
West Bridgford 22 B4
West Bromwich 21 G11
West Burton 32 F2
Westbury
  Shrops 20 F4
  Wilts 8 C3
Westbury-on-
  Severn 14 E6
Westbury-sub-
  Mendip 7 G14
West Calder 40 G3
West Coker 5 B9
Westcott 10 E2
West Dean 8 E7
West End 9 F9
Westerham 10 D5
West Felton 20 D4
Westfield 11 H9
West Grinstead 10 G2
West Haddon 22 H5
Westhill 50 G7
Westhoughton 26 E7
West Kilbride 38 F7
West Kingsdown ... 10 C6
West Kirby 26 G3
Westleton 25 J9
West Linton 40 H4

West Looe 3 F10
West Lulworth 8 K3
West Malling 10 D7
West Meon 9 E11
West Mersea 25 P5
Westminster 10 A4
West Moors 8 G5
Weston 21 D10
Weston-super-Mare . 7 E12
Westonzoyland 7 H12
West Rasen 29 F9
Westruther 41 H9
West Thorney 9 G12
Westward Ho! 6 J3
West Wellow 9 F8
West Woodburn 36 E7
Wetheral 36 H3
Wetherby 32 K6
Wetwang 33 J11
Weybourne 24 A6
Weybridge 16 J5
Weyhill 9 C8
Weymouth 5 F10
Whaley Bridge 27 G11
Whalley 27 B8
Whalton 37 E10
Whatton 22 B6
Whauphill 34 J5
Whaw 32 D1
Wheatley
  Notts 28 F6
  Oxon 15 F14
Wheatley Hill 37 K12
Wheaton Aston 21 E9
Wheldrake 33 K8
Whicham 30 F7
Whickham 37 G11
Whimple 4 D4
Whipsnade 16 D5
Whissendine 22 D7
Whitburn 40 G2
Whitby 33 C10
Whitchurch
  Bristol 14 K5
  Bucks 16 D3
  Devon 3 D12
  Hants 9 C9
  Hereford 14 E4
  Shrops 20 B6
White Bridge 48 G5
Whitehall Village . 56 D6
Whitehaven 30 C5
Whitehouse 38 D3
Whitekirk 41 E9
Whiteparish 8 E7
Whitfield 11 E14
Whithorn 34 K5
Whitland 12 E5
Whitley Bay 37 F12
Whitonditch 15 J11
Whitsome 41 H11
Whitstable 11 C12
Whitstone 3 B10
Whittington
  Derbys 28 G2
  Lancs 31 G12
  Shrops 20 C4
  Staffs 21 F12
Whittlebury 16 A1
Whittlesey 23 F11
Whittlesford 17 A9
Whitwell
  Derbys 28 G4
  IoW 9 K10
Whitwick 22 D3
Whitworth 27 D9
Whixley 32 K6
Whome 56 G3
Wick
  Hants 8 F6
  Highland 53 D15
  V Glam 13 J13
Wicken 23 H14
Wickford 17 F12
Wickham 9 G10
Wickham Market 25 K8

Wickwar 14 H6
Widdrington 37 D11
Widecombe in the
  Moor 4 F1
Widemouth Bay 3 A9
Wide Open 37 F11
Widnes 26 G6
Wigan 26 E6
Wigmore
  Hereford 20 K5
  Medway 11 C9
Wigston 22 F5
Wigton 35 J13
Wigtown 34 H5
Wilkhaven 53 K11
Willand 4 C4
Willaston 26 H4
Willenhall 21 F10
Willersley 14 B2
Willesborough 11 E11
Willingdon 10 J7
Willington
  Bedford 16 A6
  Durham 37 K10
Williton 7 H9
Willoughby 29 G13
Wilmington 4 D6
Wilmslow 27 G9
Wilnecote 21 F13
Wilton 8 D6
Wimblington 23 F13
Wimborne Minster . 8 H5
Wincanton 5 A11
Winchcombe 15 D9
Winchelsea 11 H10
Winchester 9 E9
Windermere 31 E10
Windsor 16 H4
Windygates 40 C6
Wing 16 C3
Wingate 37 K13
Wingham 11 D13
Winkleigh 3 A14
Winscombe 7 F13
Winsford 26 J7
Winslow 16 C2
Winster 27 J13
Winston 32 C3
Winterborne
  Stickland 8 G3
Winterbourne Abbas. 5 E10
Winterton
  N Lincs 29 C8
  Norf 24 C9
Wirksworth 28 J1
Wisbech 23 D13
Wisbech St Mary ... 23 D13
Wisborough Green . 10 G1
Wishaw 39 E13
Witchampton 8 G4
Witchford 23 H14
Witham 17 D13
Witheridge 4 B1
Withern 29 F13
Withernsea 29 B12
Withington 15 E9
Witley 9 D14
Witnesham 25 K6
Witney 15 E12
Wittersham 11 G10
Wiveliscombe 7 J9
Wivelsfield 10 G4
Wivenhoe 25 N5
Wix 25 N6
Woburn 16 B4
Woburn Sands 16 B4
Woking 16 K5
Wokingham 16 J3
Wolf's Castle 12 D3
Wollaston 23 J8
Wolsingham 37 K9
Wolverhampton ... 21 G10
Wolverton 16 B3
Wolviston 32 B6
Wombwell 28 E3
Wonersh 10 E1
Wonston 9 D9

Woodbridge 25 L7
Woodbury 4 E4
Woodchester 14 F7
Woodchurch 11 F10
Woodcote 16 G1
Woodgreen 8 F6
Woodhall Spa 29 H11
Woodhouse 28 F3
Woodhouse Eaves .. 22 D4
Woodley 16 H2
Woodstock 15 E13
Woofferton 20 K6
Wookey 7 G14
Wookey Hole 7 G14
Wool 8 J3
Woolacombe 6 G3
Woolavington 7 G12
Wooler 37 A8
Woolwich 10 B5
Woolwich Ferry ... 10 B5
Wooperton 37 A9
Woore 21 B8
Wootton Bassett .. 15 H9
Wootton Bridge ... 9 H10
Wootton Wawen ... 21 K12
Worcester 14 A7
Worfield 21 G8
Workington 30 B5
Worksop 28 G4
Wormit 40 A6
Worsbrough 28 D2
Wortham 24 H5
Worthing 10 J2
Wotton under Edge . 14 G6
Wragby 29 G10
Wrangle 29 J13
Wrea Green 26 B4
Wrentham 24 G9
Wretham 24 G4
Wrexham 20 A4
Writtle 17 E11
Wroughton 15 J10
Wroxham 24 D7
Wroxton 15 B13
Wyberton 23 A11
Wye 11 E11
Wylye 8 D5
Wymondham
  Leics 22 D7
  Norf 24 E6

Y

Yalding 11 E8
Yarcombe 4 C6
Yardley Hastings . 22 K7
Yarm 32 C6
Yarmouth 9 J8
Yarnton 15 E13
Yarrow 36 A2
Yate 14 H6
Yatton 7 E13
Yaxley 23 F10
Yeadon 27 A12
Yealmpton 3 F13
Yelverton 3 E13
Yeovil 5 B9
Yetminster 5 C9
Y Felinheli 18 D5
York 32 J7
Youlgreave 27 J13
Yoxall 21 E12
Yoxford 25 J8
Ysbyty Ifan 18 F8
Ysbyty Ystwyth ... 19 N7
Ystalyfera 13 F11
Ystradgynlais 13 E11

Z

Zennor 2 H2